ENDORSEMENTS

If you are a Small Business Owner, Entrepreneur or looking to start a business, this collection of real-world topics is for You. The authors' insights are "Brilliant Breakthroughs" into the world of the small business marketplace; providing a new way of conducting business that will put you onto a path of success. This book is written by small business owners, for small business owners looking to leverage the expertise of industry professionals for a fresh perspective on entrepreneurship. A definite must read for those who want access to the collaborative community of practicing experts. After 20 years of owning a small business, I have found the book that speaks to my passion for the next 20 years...and beyond!
– Timothy P. Dwyer, Small Business Owner

"Brilliant Breakthrough for the Small Business Owner" is an excellent read--practical and entertaining. I only wish it had been published in 1983 when I was starting my first company!
– John R. Howman, CEO Allied Consulting Group, Inc.
Vistage Chair

Practicing Experts is the perfect description for the contributors to Brilliant Breakthroughs. The words thought-provoking barely begin to scratch the surface of this fresh and new perspective for small business success. Working through the 4 performance pillars is effortless and provides the reader with a quantum way to look at and within their business! More than a "must read," this book is a "must do!" Brilliant Breakthroughs will without a doubt shorten the learning curve to running a successful business. Kudos to Maggie Mongan, Anthology Leader of Brilliant Breakthroughs for the Small Business Owner: Fresh Perspective on Profitability, People, Productivity, and Finding Peace in Your Business has hit a home run with both her contributors as well
as timely and intuitive nature of the content!
– Larunce Pipkin, MEd.
International #1 Bestselling author of Bankroll Your Mind

This is a much-needed book that offers a practical, forward thinking new model for the small business owner. It is a wonderful balance in how to integrate inner peace with outer profitability."
– Susan Wisehart, MS, LMFT, holistic psychotherapist in private practice and author of "Soul Visioning, Clear the Past, Create Your Future"

As an entrepreneur, I learned everything the hard way, on the job, baptism by fire, if you will. If only there was a way to learn from other's mistakes and successes. Well with this book, Brilliant Breakthroughs for the Small Business Owner, you have just that. An opportunity to learn from others; the experts on profitability, people, productivity, and peace. You'll learn what to do and more importantly what not to do. If you're one of those rare people who wants to go it alone, by starting your own business, you will find with this book that you are never truly alone because you have these experts and their experiences from which to learn.

- **George A. Santino**
Author of Get Back Up: From the Streets to Microsoft Suites

Brilliant Breakthroughs is a terrific compilation for small business owners with all the little things that become the big things. Put together in an easy to digest way, and focusing on the 4 performance pillars many small businesses need to build their business and find their way in what can be a lonely and difficult road to creating a profitable life.

– **Phil Gerbyshak**, Speaker, Author and Digital Sales Coach

Organized using the "4 Performance Pillars for Small Business Success," Brilliant Breakthroughs is an easily-readable How-To book offering keen insights for the small business owner.

– **Robert Grede**, Bestselling author of 'Naked Marketing – The Bare Essentials' [Prentice Hall]

This book is a must-read for any business owner who wants more freedom and peace of mind in their business. Business owners have been under-served in the four key areas of profitability, people, productivity and peacefulness lately. Start improving these for yourself today by using the concepts in this book.

– **Eric Levenhagen, Award-Winning Financial Coach**
Leader of Confident Wealth Building for Service Professional Entrepreneurs (Facebook Group)

I've had the pleasure of meeting all of the authors, less one. All of them are extremely knowledgeable about what they do. They all seek to deepen their knowledge to continuously become ever-more-expert at their chosen endeavors. What really astonishes is how eloquently the writers convey their subject-matter expertise in this book. The care each author gives their topic is self-evident. And the range of topics is phenomenal, perfect for proprietors of every stripe. I strongly recommend this volume to entrepreneurs and seasoned business owners alike for the competence, the sage advice, the vision, and the *heart* offered by these Brilliant Breakthroughs authors.

– **Keith Klein,** Owner/Operator, OnYourMark, LLC

As a business coach for entrepreneurs, I love Nancy Lucchesi's compelling words, "A dream fuels passion". It is spot on for anyone who wants to be successful as an entrepreneur. Without a dream, your work just becomes a job in which you are the boss. With passion, your work is the fuel that keeps your business growing year after year.
– **Kelli Sample** www.kellisample.com Sales and Business Strategist

A great book focused towards all SBO's and hopeful entrepreneurs. A book with enough reference to get your juices flowing and pumped for more. This book will guide you towards the direction of being a leader and many other tips that will lead you towards success in all areas of your life. Cool book! Recommend to anyone wanting a boost and something different! Clear, encouraging, informative, and inspirational. Get it!
– **Debbie Leoni,** Fearless Living Speaker and Coach

This is The Small Business Owner's Mastermind –
Starting a business is a lonely proposition. I know when I started my business, I felt so alone and the only advice I seemed to get regularly was from non-business owners.

Starting a business is hard. Running it profitability, well, that's even harder. The good news is with this book, you don't have to go it alone. This book really is like having your own personal small business owner mastermind. It's real advice from people who have walked in your shoes. From profitability to productivity to understanding why your current headshot image may be turning potential clients away, this book answers all of the questions you have in your mind but have not yet decided to ask.

There's no need to "go it alone" and with this book, you don't have to. I wish I had this resource when I started my business.
– **Ryan Rhoten**, CareerBrand, Inc.
Author, CareerKred - 4 Simple Steps to Build Your Digital Brand
and Boost Credibility in your Career

This book is a rare gem that speaks to the heart of a small business owner. Each one of the Brilliant Practicing Experts reveal truths and tips that other experts aren't willing or able to share with you. My two small businesses are multifaceted. The tips shared in this book have not only been gems for my business and work life, but for my personal life as well. I am grateful this book found me!
– **Lisa Marie Teubel,** BS Mgmt, MDIV

This book is full of insightful and unconventional solutions to help you transform your dream into a thriving and successful business. A must read for today's entrepreneur!
– Brynn Doering – Freelance Hair and makeup artist

Now here is a book that I can relate to. Having been in business since 2002 and now serving over 1,300 customers worldwide with proposals delivering over $16 billion in Federal awards, I am still searching for those pearls of wisdom to make my retirement more obvious. I have read many books on the topic of business best practices, and they all have something to offer, but none are anywhere near complete.

This book, although also unable to answer every business strategy survey, takes a big bite out of many of the more challenging issues. Like a business coach, a lot can be gained if you take the time to invest in your personal/business development, but be careful where you spend your time and money. Go with proven systems with a solid reputation for success. I really like the material covered in this short compendium.

It was referred to me by my professional photographer. If you are a business owner looking to build your public reputation/persona and don't have one, I strongly recommend you read her chapter, "Why Your Headshot Could be a Turn-off and How to Turn it On," and hire one. I'm sure glad I did – years ago, when I ran my first political campaign.

– Timothy Peterson, President, Federal Proposal Support Services
SalesAutomationSupport.com

BRILLIANT BREAKTHROUGHS
FOR THE SMALL BUSINESS OWNER:
Fresh Perspectives on Profitability, People, Productivity, and Finding Peace in Your Business

COMPILED BY
MAGGIE MONGAN

Brilliant Breakthroughs, Inc.
Milwaukee, WI

BRILLIANT BREAKTHROUGHS FOR THE SMALL BUSINESS OWNER:
Fresh Perspectives on Profitability, People, Productivity, and Finding Peace
in Your Business

For information contact:
Brilliant Breakthroughs, Inc.
703 Heron Drive
Waterford, WI 53185
www.BrilliantBreakthroughs.com

Book and Cover design by Maggie Mongan

ISBN-13: 978-0999437506
ISBN-10: 099943750X

First Edition: November 2017

10 9 8 7 6 5 4 3 2 1

DEDICATION

**This book is dedicated to Small Business Owners.
You are our economy's accelerant.**

CONTENTS

Acknowledgments   *XI*

Introduction   *1*

Brilliant Practicing Experts™   *6*

The 4 Performance Pillars for Small Business Success™   *7*

How to Use this Book   *9*

PERFORMANCE PILLAR 1: PROFITABILITY

Chapter One   *17*
Simplifying Small Business Success in the 21st Century
Maggie Mongan

Chapter Two   *31*
**If Your Marketing Efforts Aren't Bringing in New Clients,
Here's the 3 Step Solution**
Greg Nicholson

Chapter Three   43
Sales Suck in Solitude
Dave Wallace

PERFORMANCE PILLAR 2: PEOPLE

Chapter Four   *55*
Why Your Headshot May be a Turn-off and How to Turn It On!
Stacy Kaat

Chapter Five   *65*
**How to Avoid the 3 Most Common Challenges Every Small
Business Owner Encounters**
Mike Raber

Chapter Six   *77*
Your Voice ON AIR
Jake Nawrocki

PERFORMANCE PILLAR 3: PRODUCTIVITY

Chapter Seven   *89*
Unleash Your Mind, Unleash Your Growth!
Nancy Lucchesi

Chapter Eight   *99*
Why Small Business Owners Don't Sleep at Night
Dave Rebro

PERFORMANCE PILLAR 4: PEACEFULNESS

Chapter Nine   *113*
Hope: Out of the Shadows and Into the Light
Susan White

Chapter Ten   *123*
All Action, No Traction? Sometimes it's All in Your Head
Lori Bonaparte

CONCLUSION   *135*

COLLECTIVE BIBLIOGRAPHY   *137*

ACKNOWLEDGMENTS

Above all else, to the love of my life, Chris. You captured my heart over 35 years ago. My deepest appreciation for all the extra love and support you offered through this special project.

There are so many people to thank for stepping up and co-create this extraordinary book. Thank you, beloved contributing authors, for delivering high quality chapter content and making this journey one to remember. You definitely *Bring the WOW*!

Additional gratitude to all who stepped forward, from interviewees sharing their wisdom and endorsers offering their praise, to Lucas Robak for sparking the idea back in September 2016. Endless appreciation to our editor Clive Extence, whose keen eye and caring red pen guided our words. To an angel on earth, Laura Freund for your brilliant formatting, lay-out expertise, and swift action. Perhaps most importantly, I'm forever grateful to K. Paige Engle who appeared with a proven map to guide our actions and secure best-seller status.

I'd like to acknowledge my family for being great teachers of life, High School Teacher Ken Sadowski for teaching me how become a critical thinker, professor Mike Brandl for teaching me how to effectively debate, Dean Irene Kramer and professor Romwald Maczka of Carthage College who taught me learning is enriched through world view experiences, and Cardinal Stritch University's Instructor Clive Extence who pushed me to excel.

How can I not mention my dear mentors and friends who have traveled with and formed me through this journey we call life? Thank you: Keith Klein, Ron Chandler, Lisa Teubel, Bruce Carse, Dave Walter, Sue Lea, A. Drayton Boylston, Pat Pendergast, and Meg McNally.

Brilliant Breakthroughs for the Small Business Owner:

Fresh Perspectives on Profitability, People, Productivity, and Finding Peace in Your Business

INTRODUCTION

THE BRILLIANT QUESTION:
Maggie, why are you writing a book?

When speaking with George A. Santino, a retired Microsoft Partner and Serial Entrepreneur, he stated, "The American Dream is alive and well. You can start at the bottom and work hard. If you do, anything is achievable" (personal communication, July 7, 2017). I whole-heartedly agree with George, who is the personification of The American Dream.

THE BRILLIANT ANSWER:
Contemporary business requires small business owners to think and act differently than they did in the 20th century. Small businesses of the 21st century must find the balancing act between traditional business basics and unconventional techniques. This isn't as easy as it appears. There is a noticeable disconnect between the support system (trainers, coaches, mentors, etc.) for small business and what small business owners need to survive and thrive.

This book shares fresh perspectives in profitability, people, productivity, and peacefulness, for you to experiment with by applying them to your business. Our goal is to support small business owners in finding their potential solutions to develop their winning formula of business success.

THE BRILLIANT REASON:
The American Dream is a viable reality in this century. It provides equal opportunity for all who pursue their dream. Those who create right actions, which are spurred from right thoughts, will reap the rewards.

Many people will start a business. Most are *wantrepreneurs* (those who talk about business ownership, but don't do the work to build and deliver a successful business). This book is created for those who are seriously committed to doing the work and gaining prosperity. Ready for the good news? You can stop banging your head against the wall and quit working all hours of the night. This book is filled with all sorts of fresh perspectives for you to experiment with to find your personal secret to success.

In *The Entrepreneur's Solution*, Mel Abraham wrote, "This country was built on principles of entrepreneurialism, equity, self-determination, and opportunity. Fulfilling our potential, as individuals and as a nation is simply a matter then of reawakening that innate spirit" (Abraham, 2015, p. 3). The American Dream evolved through settlers, who became entrepreneurs and small business owners. These early founders of The American Dream started their businesses out of necessity. Some thrived to build great businesses, while others dwindled. All had the entrepreneurial spirit. Those who excelled learned how to master small business success.

Let's fast-forward to this century. If you are a seriously committed and growth focused Small Business Owner, we know you're seeking new ways to:

- become more profitable
- develop better quality working relationships with your team and others
- explore and experiment with new productivity practices and tools
- find more peace within your business.

Why? For you to build a profitable business and experience a more joyful and fulfilling life. We get it and you do too! We wrote this book to share some of our best practices and unconventional techniques to successfully grow YOUR Business. It's amazing what comes out of the mouths of Practicing Experts when they are sharing their wisdom.

The 21st century requires Small Business Owners (SBOs) to think and work differently to gain wins. When you are playing a new board game you usually read the rules to the game, don't you? Sure you do. Why? You want to assure you improve your probability of winning. Business is the same. There are basic rules for all businesses. We know these rules support strong business.

What's the difference in the rules for small business success between last and this century? The internet and technological advancement. Good, bad, or indifferent, the internet has both helped and hindered small business success. The internet has created endless opportunity for SBOs to share their offerings with the world. Conversely, the internet is filled with a plethora of information – useful, accurate, and inaccurate. In a short period of time, humankind has become gluttons of information.

Even with the technological advancements, many business basics are still required. In the 21st century businesses still need marketing, sales, customers, systems, accounting, etc. for business operations to run effectively and efficiently. Technology adds another layer of simplicity and complexity to any small business operation.

Technology provides opportunities for:

- greater reach to expand a business's marketplace
- around the clock promotion via social media and online advertising
- more information to consume
- efficiencies
- perpetual distractions via *Bright Shiny Objects* popping up

- more Experts and UN-Experts vying for your attention and money.

A new learning curve and balancing act for this century's SBO is far different than last century. It is a necessity for small business to swiftly secure success. Today's SBOs are required to immediately work with experts to shave years off their learning curve to secure their position in the marketplace. When SBOs take consistent actions to secure profitability, they move beyond surviving. See surprising statistics of small business survival in Chapter 1.

Today's wide-reaching arm of the internet introduces you to an infinite number of service providers to help you grow your business. **Warning:** All providers are not created equally.

There are plenty of experts in the marketplace. Experts are experienced and knowledgeable in a particular topic. Experts are masterful because they are practiced in their expertise or focused specialty.

Today's SBO has plenty of experts and UN-experts approaching them. The UN-experts are in strong force and you've probably engaged with them – vowing to never again. The UN-expert is usually an expert at online marketing, but not an expert at whatever it is they're offering. They promote well and engage you enough to secure your purchase. Unfortunately, their expertise stops there. They don't deliver at an expert level whatever the topic is you bought. The UN-expert tends to keep their customers in a state of mediocrity or perpetual need for their services.

Good news! You don't have to settle for UN-experts. In fact, a group of us believes SBOs deserve much better than what the marketplace is commonly providing for support. Over the past 18 months, I have been selecting and vetting Practicing Experts. There are many Practicing Experts in the marketplace. Those who are willing to openly share how they blend their best practices and unconventional techniques to build winning strategies and practical tactics to amplify their business success are collaborating authors of this book.

Some of you may ask, "How do you know they're practicing experts Maggie?" For almost a decade, I had the honor of being trained to be one to the industry's top performers, as an Executive Recruiter and Certified Senior Account Manager, specializing in placing Change Agents into organizations. Additionally, I've coached executives, SBOs, non-profit leaders, and other professional coaches for 20 years. Last, I've been coaching SBOs for approximately 15 years.

In the late 1990s, I started saying to all the Change Agents I was recruiting, "It's all about being an Agent of Change; not an Agent for Change." Over the years I've refined this to, "Don't be an agent for change; be the agent OF change." As you can see, I am an advocate for appropriate change. How successful business was conducted in the 1990s and even 2000s isn't enough for today's small business. Change – appropriate change, is required for SBOs to succeed in business. Most SBOs already know this, but they are unsure what to do about it.

This perplexed me too! For the past 4 years I've been seeking a solution. What is it you ask? You're reading it. I invited other experts to build a collaborative community of

Brilliant Practicing Experts™ to bring proven and effective fresh perspectives to Small Business Owners. To reveal our commitment level to you, we started a mobile app named *Brilliant* to support this book's readers. This book is the first book in an annual series designed to continue giving you different fresh perspectives to experiment with throughout the years.

All this has me singing the lyrics to the original *Ghostbusters* movie, "Who ya gonna call?" Hopefully your answer isn't the slick marketers who will be ghosted next year but it is to engage with Brilliant Practicing Experts™ once you read their chapter. Why? This is how you will learn this century's winning formula of success.

Tip: Most, not all, UN-experts keep you in a state of mediocre busy-ness work. Why? When you only gain mediocre results, you still need them and will pay them more money to get additional mediocre results. Even though they say otherwise, many UN-experts want you to become only moderately successful.

I know, that behavior is not acceptable! Since we are a society who is addicted to being busy, this has become a perfect storm for many online marketers. Unfortunately, they are capitalizing on this and robbing you of your profitability, productivity, and finding peace in your business.

What's the better approach to 21st century small business success?

Blending Best Practices and technology to create unconventional approaches. Why? Guided by a Brilliant Practicing Expert™, this approach will provide you and your business unconventional results. Brilliant Practicing Experts™ focus on attracting customers (catch), teach you what you need to learn so you can do it independently from them (feed), then encourage you to experiment with your new teachings (release), and are available if you need assistance (support).

Remember: Some information on the internet is accurate and some is inaccurate. If it was about having access to information, wouldn't we all be rich, physically fit, and beautiful by now? **Clue:** We are currently experiencing an information surplus and a deficit of application.

Your business's success is dependent upon you (1) securing the appropriate information, and (2) learning how to appropriately apply it to your business's circumstances. Today's SBO has a variety of options available of what to offer and a myriad of delivery alternatives. Some techniques better support certain types of expertise or customers. There is a plethora of success options to consider; yet, some might not support your business as well as others.

How do you learn which approach is best? Experiment. The United States of America was founded by immigrants who learned how to support themselves through entrepreneurial activities and developing small businesses. Those who practiced until they succeeded built growing business. Eventually, some of them became founding businesses of America. These early founders of The American Dream understood the value of experimenting.

Everything was new to these early business experimenters. The Founders of American Business needed to swiftly try new approaches and learn which ones did or didn't deliver favorable gains. Those who found success strategies and techniques became prosperous. Those who didn't find business success may not have survived.

The 21st century may not have mortality attached to business success for most as it did in the 16th and 17th century, but it still requires an unwavering commitment from the SBO. The commitment is one of first surviving and then thriving. This requires and invites SBOs endless exploring and experimenting to find favorable results for their business. Those who persistently take action win. Those who take action on the right things win BIG.

Gary Vaynerchuk, high profile American Serial Entrepreneur often referred to as GaryVee, is known by his followers for advocating action. He frequently references hustling. Often you hear him say things like, "Work, that's how you get it", "Stop crying; keep hustling", or "Without hustle, talent will only carry you so far". Vaynerchuk is a proponent of taking action and experimentation to shorten an entrepreneur's learning curves.

On a July 7, 2017 Instagram Live (https://www.instagram.com/garyvee/) GaryVee said, "Entrepreneurship emerges as culture". The culture, he elaborated about is one of action. He encouraged *wantrepreneurs* to be practical and appropriately prepare for their business by gaining tutelage before and during entrepreneurship. He also emphasized a business's success rate is improved through experimentation – just like the early founders of The American Dream.

Typically, right thoughts and right actions deliver favorable results. Some, not all, of the Best Practices of corporations are favorable for small business success. Conversely there are many strategies, techniques, mindsets, and behaviors that would become unfavorable if scaled to larger organizations.

I still notice many former corporate employees, who were downsized during this century's Great Recession, either trying to behave corporate in a small business setting, or act as if they are hyperallergic to anything which *feels* it came from their former corporate setting. I encourage former corporate folks to quit sabotaging themselves and step into small business ownership with a clean slate to improve your business's success rate.

Caution: Similar to corporate settings, the behaviors which secured your promotion aren't the same actions and behaviors that will help you break into the next level of success – there's different game plans for each level. The rules change when you change levels. The game is played differently to excel in each new level. Small business success doesn't promote its business owners. Instead, it secures scalability or another level of expansion for the business.

NOW WHAT?

Are you a committed Small Business Owner who seeks ways to make your small business more profitable and peace-filled so you can further step into living your potential? If so, you are going to enjoy this book. Figure 1 is a photo of our 2017 Brilliant Practicing Experts™ Author Team, less Lori Bonaparte.

Figure 1.

Brilliant Practicing Experts™ 2017 Team of Brilliant Breakthroughs for the Small Business Owner: Fresh Perspectives on Profitability, People, Productivity, and Finding Peace in Your Business.

Source: Brilliant Breakthroughs, Inc. Photo taken by Stacy Kaat Photography.

This extra-ordinary team has created this book (2017 version) for you to explore and experiment with fresh perspectives to improve your business's performance.

We have organized our chapter topics into **The 4 Performance Pillars for Small Business Success**™ model: Profitability, People, Productivity, and Peacefulness. Over the past 2 decades of serving businesses, I've noticed all business activities can be categorized into these 4 categories or Performance Pillars. The size and industry of a business doesn't alter this model.

When you review **The 4 Performance Pillars for Small Business Success**™ model (see Figure 2), you will see The 4 Performance Pillars in the center. I have added two columns for you to discern where you or your business may need to strengthen a Performance Pillar.

The column on the left, *Experience this when I DON'T have it* column gives you key words to assess if you are lacking (or not). The column on the right, *Experience this when I DO have it* column reveals if you have been working these areas of your business effectively. The key is to fortify each of the 4 Performance Pillars. The following is a brief description of each of The 4 Performance Pillars.

Figure 2.

THE 4 PERFORMANCE PILLARS FOR SMALL BUSINESS SUCCESS™

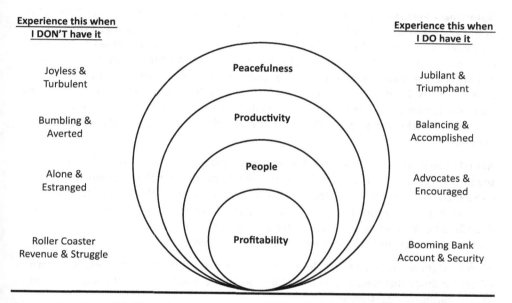

Experience this when
I DON'T have it

Joyless &
Turbulent

Bumbling &
Averted

Alone &
Estranged

Roller Coaster
Revenue & Struggle

Peacefulness

Productivity

People

Profitability

Experience this when
I DO have it

Jubilant &
Triumphant

Balancing &
Accomplished

Advocates &
Encouraged

Booming Bank
Account & Security

Source: Courtesy of Brilliant Breakthroughs Inc., Simplify Small Business Success Program: https://academy.brilliantbreakthroughs.com/

Performance Pillar 1: Profitability

The primary determinant of Business Success is if your business is profitable. We train on these topics: financials, product development, sales, marketing, branding, operations, business models, your business's purpose-vision-mission for alignment, and anything related to profit.

Performance Pillar 2: People

People are what makes the world go around – and your business too. We train on these topics: effective networking, social media, team development, employees, your business's ideal customer, business allies (joint ventures, etc.), customers, and anything related to relationship building and people.

Performance Pillar 3: Productivity

Productivity practices can make or break a business. Simplifying your activities may be easier than what you're making it out to be. We train on these topics: time management (which really doesn't exist), simplifying techniques, automated systems, tech and apps to support us being more effective and efficient, and anything related to productivity.

Performance Pillar 4: Peacefulness

Peacefulness is a possibility when you have a mindful and profitable business. It isn't necessary to polarize peace and profit. Peace is one of the elusive elements of Business Success that doesn't need to be far-fetched. We train on these topics: self-management, balanced leadership and self-leadership, utilizing core values, daily practices, mindset, overall well-being, and anything related to peaceful prosperity.

Note: The 4 Performance Pillars for Small Business Success™ model is one of the Small Business's Evolution. It illustrates how Profitability anchors your business. Profit is always at the forefront. Since people decide whether to make a purchase or not, People is the next essential ring surrounding Profit. There are many moving parts that need attention while conducting business. Learning how to be effective and efficient are essential; thus, Productivity is the next ring after People. The more People involved, the more Productivity becomes a focus. People don't want to, nor should they, work in an unpeaceful workplace. Peace is the outer ring, which encapsulates all the other activities.

At first glance, many SBOs will see this as I described. At another glance, SBOs may say the sequence could be reversed. This is the beauty of this model. Depending on your current business performance focus, you could move any one of the 4 pillars around since each pillar integrates with all the others. **Hint:** I do suggest you work the model as described because you can have all the peace you'd like to have, but if you don't have profit, your peace and business won't be lasting too long.

It's our intention to help you explore fresh perspectives in each of **The 4 Performance Pillars for Small Business Success**™ to have brilliant breakthroughs for yourself as well as your business's performance.

WHAT'S NEXT?

Before our Brilliant Practicing Experts™ bring you the WOW! in each of their chapters, please take a moment to learn how the book is designed for you to use as a guide. Also, please engage with us on our mobile app: **BrilliantBizBook**. You may be surprised what we have there. Have some fun experimenting and shining brightly!

Brilliant Breakthroughs for the Small Business Owner
HOW TO USE THIS BOOK

This book is a compilation or anthology of 10 authors, who are Brilliant Practicing Experts™, willing to share their wisdom and winning formulas with you, the small business owner.

As you read the book, you may notice it feels as if you are reading 10 different books. Why? Each chapter was written by a different author. Out of respect to each author, who has already created their customer base and a communication style within their marketplace, we honored their communication style throughout their chapter. We prefer this approach because we want you to know exactly what to expect when you reach out to engage with our authors.

This book is designed to introduce and wisdom-share fresh perspectives so you may create some brilliant breakthroughs for yourself and your business's performance. Use this book as a guide over the next year. Whatever you do, please don't only read this book and put it on the shelf! Instead we invite you to experiment with the new ideas presented here. Learn and apply, practice and tweak, and then when you have a new best practice, smile and share your good news with us!

What you won't find in this book is advertisements. No one will be pitching their products or services to you. Our goal is to wisdom-share fresh perspectives for small business success.

BOOK LAYOUT:

This book's layout is organized via *The 4 Performance Pillars for Small Business Success*™ described in the Introduction.

Performance Pillar 1: Profitability

Chapter 1:

Simplifying Small Business Success in the 21st Century
by Maggie Mongan

Simplifying your business's success isn't easy, but it can be simple. Small business is shrouded with inaccurate and misguiding myths that may lead owners into actions, which may not serve their business's performance best. Do you know we are living in a unique time when The American Dream is alive and well while we're simultaneously experiencing America's Entrepreneurial Epidemic? Learn how to experiment with **The 4 Performance Pillars for Small Business**™. Discover insights, tips, clues, and questions to help you discern how to improve your performance and your small business's performance.

Chapter 2:

If Your Marketing Efforts Aren't Bringing in New Clients, Here's the 3-Step Solution
by Greg Nicholson

If your marketing efforts aren't effectively supporting your revenue expectations something is off with your marketing approach. Small business owners usually focus on the marketing tactics and then wonder why they aren't generating enough sales. Most of the time it isn't the tactics that are failing. Marketing strategies are missing. Without understanding and creating a strong marketing strategy your marketing tactics will fall short.

If your efforts aren't bringing new clients you will appreciate this walk-though of the 3 key elements to creating a predictable Client Generation System:

1. Ideal Client Profile

2. Market Dominating Position

3. The Conversion Equation

Chapter 3:

Sales Suck in Solitude
by Dave Wallace

Bike riding and Business-to-Business sales. They don't seem to have much in common. Or, do they? To the casual observer, both look like solitary activities. Cyclists generate all their own power and do it all themselves, right? The same with sellers. They have to learn their products and/or services, prospect for customers, make cold calls, meet with clients, create proposals, on and on.

In his chapter, David Wallace shares a personal cycling story and draws parallels to selling, demonstrating that sometimes appearances can be deceiving. Cycling, and selling, as it turns out, are far from individual activities.

Performance Pillar 2: People

Chapter 4:

Why Your Headshot May be a Turn-off and How to Turn It On!
by Stacy Kaat

Your headshot is your first impression. It can make or break your chances of getting a job, promotion, a customer's business, or even a date. In a saturated marketplace, how can you turn people on to you and your product or service? Learn how to use your headshot to showcase your unique personality, become memorable, and rise above the noise. This chapter addresses the importance of utilizing your headshot to effectively communicate what you want others to know about you, finding the right photographer, and releasing headshot fear, so you can focus on your message and attract the right people.

Chapter 5:

How to Avoid the 3 Most Common Challenges Every Small Business Owner Encounters
by Mike Raber

All great businesses share three simple disciplines. Throughout this chapter, we explore some of the core challenges small business owners face. We also discover the many solutions of how to avoid having your business derailed by these challenges. This is a must read for all small business owners. I will share the importance of developing consistent systematized lead generation, working as a team, and having a financial/business plan in place. "By ourselves we can do great things, yet together we can climb the highest mountain. Together we can change the world for the better."

Chapter 6:

Your Voice ON AIR
by Jake Nawrocki

Podcasting is arguably the best and most unique place to hang your shingle today. With over a billion listeners and only a few hundred thousand shows, listeners are excited to hear how your business and value can help them. This chapter will open your eyes to see what you have been missing in your current business. Podcasting will build relationships, create credibility, and bring in more customers. Creating a podcast may not be in your current plan, but I suggest you read, learn, and take action because this will create the best impact for your business to date.

Performance Pillar 3: Productivity

Chapter 7:

Unleash Your Mind, Unleash Your Growth!
by Nancy Lucchesi

Sometimes our biggest obstacles are our own thoughts. Remarkable things start to happen when you make just the slightest adjustments. Do you set goals every year? Learn how to empower and fuel your goals to achieve success. Do you feel you must do everything yourself to thrive? You'll read how to do what you do best and hire the rest. Embrace technology and use it to explode your business. You will see there is more than one way to view things. Unleash your own power by unleashing your mind. Amazing growth happens when you do.

Chapter 8:

Why Small Business Owners Don't Sleep at Night
by Dave Rebro

As small business owners, entrepreneurs and solopreneurs, our minds can become cluttered with decisions, appointments, tasks, projects, clients, and challenges from both our business and personal lives. Too much clutter in our mind and workspace can overwhelm us with stress, anxiety, confusion, and most of all, lack of sleep.

Reading this chapter, you'll learn simple and effective strategies to prepare you for a productive day, help declutter your mind and workspace, block time for your highest payoff activities, and help you maintain focus on what's most important to you in business and in life.

Performance Pillar 4: Peacefulness

Chapter 9:

Hope: Out of the Shadows and Into the Light
by Susan White

The concept of "hope" is ambiguous, abstract, and can sometimes be confused with creating a strategy for success in a small business setting. Transforming it into something more concrete supports personal enlightenment, as well as increasing the likelihood of financial success. When hope's influence unconsciously resides in the shadows of our minds, it may limit profitability and capabilities. Other times, it may conflict with valuable aspects of who we are and can distract or sabotage us from taking much-needed action. Thought-provoking enlightenment for those of us who own or manage a small business is the intention of this chapter!

Chapter 10:

All Action, No Traction? Sometimes it's All in Your Head
by Lori Bonaparte

Pursuing your business goals can become a form of self-expression and a source of financial livelihood. Contained within your business is a customized personal development program specifically designed for you. Knowing how to use your gifts, talents, and strengths to create a better version of yourself, will naturally increase your business success.

If you're experiencing a lot of action and little traction in reaching your business goals, there are three critical elements that could be responsible. The challenges you face may seem as if they're in the environment, but the answer to them is usually found within your mind.

CHAPTER LAYOUT:

Introduction to the Chapters' Brilliant Practicing Expert™
As the Anthology Leader, Maggie will introduce you to each chapter's author. She shares what makes the author unique via their skills and capabilities. Additionally, you will learn why the chapter's topic, through the lens of the author, matters to your business's performance.

Chapter Writing
Chapters are filled with tenured wisdom, tips, and experiences relevant to Small Business Owners (SBOs). We encourage you to learn and experiment to find your winning formula.

Chapter Glossary
All Brilliant Practicing Experts™ have terms they use in a particular fashion. Each chapter has a glossary to clarify what the author means as they impart their wisdom.

Author Biography Page
Each author wants you to become familiar with them. Included is a headshot, brief author description, and an invitation to connect with them further.

Business Page
Each author's business is represented with an informative page for you to become more familiar with the author's business. It contains a brief business description, and links for you to connect on their website and their social media accounts.

ADDITIONAL RESOURCES:

Book Purchases
This book is sold through Amazon.com and personally through each of the authors. For bulk orders, please contact Maggie Mongan at https://www.brilliantbreakthroughs.com/contact-us/.

To learn more about the authors, please go to:
https://www.brilliantbreakthroughs.com/book-2017/

Here you can meet all the authors online. Each Author's Landing Page contains information about them and their business, as well as podcast interviews, videos, and social media links.

We also invite you to engage with us via our mobile app: BrilliantBizBook

Here you will find similar content to the Author's Landing Page as well as: new podcasts, blogs, events, new products and offerings, tips, tricks, and wisdom-sharings. You have us on demand in the palm of your hand once you access our mobile app!

Enjoy these fresh perspectives, meeting some Brilliant Practicing Experts™, and shining brightly!

**Performance
Pillar 1**

PROFITABILITY

Brilliant Breakthroughs for the Small Business Owner

Allow Me to Introduce Brilliant Practicing Expert™ Maggie Mongan by Keith Klein

Maggie Mongan does not march to the beat of a different drummer.

Instead, she combines these qualities into an entire orchestra:

- abundant practical experience getting proven results,
- personal and professional commitments to excellence,
- genuine interests in helping others plus a drive to succeed,
- passion for discovering and sharing peace and joy, and
- considerable analysis and reflection.

She doesn't march to that orchestra, either. She dances to it!

Maggie's rare combination of pragmatic pursuits - coupled with an incessant quest for finding opportunities for joy in all situations - makes Maggie one of the most genuine people I know.

Here's a great insight about Maggie: she practices what she preaches.

Maggie outlines her 4 Pillars of Performance for you here. If you get to know her, in print or in person, you'll recognize a friend, a mentor, and a champion of (your) business. Read it. Create and take actions on each Pillar. Enjoy it! Then, help other small business owners by encouraging them to do the same, pillar by pillar, and then share with others.

Simplifying Small Business Success in the 21st Century
by Maggie Mongan

The 21st century small business owner has boundless opportunities available to achieve staggering success. Last century's technological innovations supported the growth of the Small Business Movement. This century's proliferation of social media has amplified the capability for all businesses to reach a larger audience. Today's swift pace technology provides opportunities to scale business as we have never seen before. The old way of conducting business is no longer adequate to achieve success. This leads the modern day Small Business Owner (SBO) on a new path for learning how to succeed in business.

For several decades, I've actively been involved with both corporate and small business operations morphing into 21st century businesses via adopting and adapting their technology, talent, and workflows. Some have achieved this successfully, while others are still attempting to do so. Achieving transformation for an individual is a phenomenal accomplishment, so just imagine the challenge it presents for any organization.

Note: One of the greatest competitive advantages small business has over corporate is agility.

Agility, or flexibility, provides freedom. This very freedom, which is a competitive advantage for a SBO, can become a constraint. There is a delicate balancing act each SBO must perform. Achieving business goals requires you to being mentally present. It invites you to lead your business in the direction required to land at its destination. A destination you selected.

SMALL BUSINESS FACTS

This century has witnessed an entrepreneurial explosion in the United States. According to the 2016 Annual Report of U. S. Small Business Administration:

- In 2013, there were 28.8 million small businesses.
- In 2013, microbusiness (defined as 1-9 employees) are most common.
- In 2014, the survival rate of new businesses was 79.9%.
- During 2004-2014, 78.5% of new establishments survived one year.

Statistical Note: These statistics are based on small businesses which have formally created a business entity and submit annual filings to the Internal Revenue Service.

Yes, you read this correctly. The myth that 50% of all businesses don't survive the first year of business is false. If you are a SBO, who has survived year one of conducting business, you have a good deal of company. Congratulations – get up and do your happy dance!

Survival of year one is favorable. Yet, the statistic reflects survival instead of businesses thriving. SBOs are commonly known to have financial struggles. For over a dozen years,

I have been observing and researching this. Are you curious about what I've discovered regarding small business success?

AMERICA'S ENTREPRENEURIAL EPIDEMIC

Disclaimer: The above Small Business Facts, are only representing formally created businesses. America's Entrepreneurial Epidemic also includes all people who operated informal businesses, AKA: not formally recognized through government agencies.

There is a very real Entrepreneurial Epidemic in our country: There are small business owners who *romanticize* business ownership. Typically, they are neglecting the business's needs and stunting its growth. You don't have to be chained to your business to be successful, but you do need to tend to the needs of your business.

Are you wondering if you're a SBO who romanticizes versus rolls up your sleeves and does the work? Allow me to describe how the romancing SBO appears to others. The lovers of small business ownership are the ones who usually show up at all the networking events, have lunches or coffees consistently scheduled, and will do dinner or other events with other business owners. Doesn't this sound like a seriously committed small business owner who is trying to build their business? Yes, it does – and it is.

Now let me share the rest of the story. Some of these are SBOs complain about financially investing in their business or professional development for themselves to become a better business leader. They say they don't have money to grow their business. They usually gripe about how busy they are or how they must learn new technology, etc., to grow their business. Are you ready for the kicker? They also complain they don't have enough customers, time, and money.

Most of these romanticizing SBOs have a love/hate relationship with their business. Worse yet, they may not even know this is their truth. They glamorize the *feel-good* aspects of business and loath the work of business ownership. What do they end up with? A business which isn't providing the financial security. You may hear them blame others, systems, or organizations because their business is failing. In reality, it is they who are failing their business.

Over the decades of being a master business coach and strategist, as well as a small business owner, I've experimented with many different strategies and tactics. I'm sure you have done this many times too. Shouldn't we always look for better ways to move the appropriate performance needles?

When I found techniques, which delivered favorable results in my business, I asked my clients to try those new strategies or tactics. What did we learn? We learned to create solid proven techniques, which delivered a productively profitable and peace-filled business. A productively profitable business is one that has a plan for developing profit through systems or automation. A peace-filled business is one that is conducting purpose-driven business, which is conducive for humans to be producing at their potential.

GRAND EXPERIMENTING OF SMALL BUSINESS OWNERS

Conducting small business is nothing more than a grand experiment. The Introduction of this book shares more about The Grand Experiment of America and entrepreneurialism. If you haven't read it yet, please do.

Every SBO wants to believe their business is unique. **Myth Buster:** Your business is not unique. How you deliver your expertise may be quite unique; however, your business is not. All businesses function the same – even nonprofit organizations function similarly.

Experimenting with different techniques within Small Businesses has revealed to me there are four key areas of performance. I name these *The 4 Performance Pillars for Small Business Success* ™. Actions that favorably impact business (power moves) are created when SBOs apply The 4 Performance Pillars to business.

PERFORMANCE PILLAR 1: PROFITABILITY

Are you ready for this? All businesses require expenses. Additionally, all businesses must create revenue. The goal, or it should be a goal, is to create greater revenue than expenses If revenue is greater than expenses a profit is created. The IRS defines a successful business as one which creates profit.

When SBOs find ways to simplify their small business success, they enjoy conducting business. Business profit is the reward for doing good business. When SBOs simplified their business, they improve their profit.

Profit is the elemental core of each business. Please note: I didn't say "profit at any cost." Unless you have a personal benefactor, you will not be able to stay in business without profit. Profit is the lifeblood of your business. George Santino, Retired Microsoft Partner and Serial Entrepreneur, proclaims, "The ultimate goal for every business is to make profit with whatever you are selling." (personal communications, July 7, 2017)

Primary Goal for Small Business: Create Profit

Secondary Goal for Small Business: Sustain Profit

Unfortunately, most SBOs don't comprehend how to actualize this. Thus, they are unprofitable and won't be able to stay in business long term.

CPA Eric Levenhagen urges SBOs to change their traditional profit equation from "Sales – Expenses = Profit" to placing profit at the beginning of the equation. He states, "It's time we change the financial behavioral system and mindset of how to attain profit. Profit is the focus. When profit is taken out of revenue first, the focus needs to shift to working with a true cashflow. Then expenses can be worked out of the cashflow" (personal communications, June 14, 2017). If your small business is not able to sustain itself, you won't be able to serve people.

While speaking with George A. Santino, he shared a great start-up tip: Do all your homework upfront, because once you open those doors – there's no turning back.

PERFORMANCE PILLAR 2: PEOPLE

Without people, your business will perish. This applies to all businesses. Even a small business whose customer base is another business needs people. People make purchasing decisions. A SBO must develop good relationship skills and customer service to assure their ability to sell and close business in order to generate revenue.

There are five types of people your business needs to have ongoing relationship with for continued growth:

Team: Either in-house or external (outsourced) or a combination of the two

Customer: Actual paying customers or potential customers (prospects)

Guidance Team: Mentors/Advisors/Coaches

Networking Hubs: These are people of influence who connect you to the right folks

Business Allies: Other folks who can help you expand your business (Joint Venture Partners, etc.)

Jason Weseman, President of FocalPoint Business Coaching of Wisconsin reveals, "People are the only strategic advantage companies have and the only real way you're going to grow your business." Jason further discussed the power of building the right team to assure business success. As a former Executive Recruiter, I couldn't agree with him more.

Weseman spoke further about the much-overlooked approach to hiring people for your in-house team or outsourcing talent. He discussed the importance of being flexible while hiring – especially with the shortage of available talent. Most likely the person you are looking for is already doing the job you need them to do. "They may not have the exact qualifications you want, but if they've done the job, they're capable of doing the job you need them to do" (personal communications, June 22, 2017). Why is this important? SBOs are afraid to hire good people with good skills and capabilities. Move beyond your requirements list and engage with people who you can develop into great teammates for your business.

Remember: Continuously developing relationships with the five types of people you need to support your business's growth could feel like a full-time job. Today, we're capable of building relationships virtually. Today's businesses are blessed with a plethora of high-tech options to make relationship building easier than in the past.

Relationship Caution: Don't get caught solely being a high-tech relationship builder. Remember to connect – be high touch as often as it makes sense. Absolutely nothing beats having face-to-face time to build lasting depth into relationships.

PERFORMANCE PILLAR 3: PRODUCTIVITY

Productivity often gets a bad reputation. There is a significant difference between productivity and *busyness*. Today, people are addicted to busy. Ask people, "How are you?" Chances are they will respond with "busy." Of course, this isn't what you asked at all! When did we become a society hooked on being busy?

Productivity is quite different from busy. Most SBOs are infected by the busyness bug. They are not accomplishing what needs to be done to accomplish business success. Why? SBOs are distracted and lack clarity. They don't have clarity of their Business Purpose, Vision, or Mission. Some SBOs behave similar to a small fishing boat drifting to the whims of the sea.

When a Small Business Owner gracefully expresses what their business offers, my heart jumps for joy. Why? They aren't floundering. They know their game plan and which actions to take. When SBOs can express the purpose of their business, their productivity is focused on their destination. I admit there isn't anything sexy about why we open the doors in the morning. However, we become very attractive when we are able to express the impact our offerings provide to our customers. It's unfortunate that most SBOs unable to speak with clarity at this level.

Defining your Business's Purpose, Vision, and Mission, allows you to know what your business's destination is and what you must do to achieve it. Each destination within a business, requires different tools and practices to assure success. Productivity helps SBOs become more effective and efficient. It's essential for you to have a well-defined process. I have never known *winging it* to be a sustainable model for success.

Productivity Clue: Customers do not care about your process unless they are process people as well. What they do care about is what they can attain once you help them resolve whatever is currently agitating them. When you have a system, your client attraction, engagement, conversion, and service becomes effective and efficient. You can generate more revenue when you have efficient processes to serve your customers. Effective customer servicing requires a streamlined process. Simplifying your business process to service your customer more effectively, makes your business more efficient.

Now I know that some of you are saying, "Great, but what can I do with my own performance to be more productive?"

Productivity Tip 1: Be the *King or Queen of Cushion*. Instead of rushing from one appointment or project to another, create a cushion of time for maybe 10-15 minutes between your commitments. This way you are more likely to complete one task before moving to the next without the stress of rushing and making excuses for running behind.

Productivity Tip 2: Before you do anything else, tackle the one task you perceive as the most frustrating or difficult. You perceive this one task as the worst thing you need to accomplish for the day. When you avoid what must be completed, you dread it even more. Eventually it becomes larger than life and a mental distraction. The enormity of this tip is understated. To share its significance, Brian Tracy wrote a book dedicated to this topic, *Eat that Frog!* (2001). This is a must read for SBOs.

Productivity Tip 3: Make appointments on your calendar for the projects or work you need to complete. Don't bump these for other appointments. Your business is a priority too.

Remember: As the most valuable team member of your business, you don't want to burn out your brilliance!

PERFORMANCE PILLAR 4: PEACE

This performance pillar always surprises SBOs; yet, it's the one thing every human strives to achieve. How often do you see SBOs, who are totally rocking their business; yet, they aren't peaceful? Conversely, how often do you see SBOs who are all about the kumbaya of generating peace and they are not profitable?

In both cases, my heart weeps when I see this. Why? It is completely unnecessary. You truly can build a thriving business which is both profitable and peace-filled. I know it is possible!

Phil Gerbyshak, Co-Founder of Vengreso states, "The key is not to balance, rather to be balancing. Making continuous and intentional actions to be balancing and reconfiguring your relationships: customers, employees, and your family" (personal communication, July 5, 2017). The concept of balance is an illusion.

Even in ancient times, the masters taught how life is filled with opportunities to find peace through mindfulness. When we are mindful, we are in constructive action. By slowing down we have the mental clarity to take the right actions.

Peace Question 1: Are you being mindful? According to Chaplain Lisa Teubel, "When a SBO and their team has peace in their hearts and minds, it will naturally flow to their families, employees, and customers while supporting an abundant bottom line" (personal communications, August 7, 2017).

Peace Question 2: How do you create peace in your small business? Do you give yourself breaks throughout the day? It is possible to be successful and have a joyful life. For most SBOs, it's found somewhere between working Tim Ferriss' "4-hour Work Week" (2009) and a 60-hour work week.

Peace Question 3: Do you have self-direction through managing your actions and schedule? You are the one in control. You decide how and when you will show up. This is one I struggle with at times. I am disciplined and a high achiever; however, I must admit my workaholic tendencies creep in far too often. Several times throughout the year I need to remind myself to chill out! Yes, I do have reminders on my calendar to help me with this.

Peace Question 4: Do you have clarity of what your business is manifesting? CPA Eric Levenhagen shares, "Change your definition of business success according to what you want from your business. It takes money to support your mission. Your profitable business can serve the greater good. Your business profit is supporting your purpose" (personal communications, June 14, 2017).

An essential goal for each SBO is to simplify. The highly successful SBOs you admire have already worked through something similar to *The 4 Performance Pillars for Small Business Success* [TM]. They simplified their small business to become successful. This doesn't have to complicated. You can achieve this as well, with incremental action steps.

NEXT STEPS

Honestly ask yourself how you are showing up to support your business's success. Is your business failing? Are you failing? Are you settling?

Conversely, is your bank account increasing? Are you smooth sailing because your relationships are bringing people into a simplified business process? What about your work load? Is it working you or are you working it? Last, and perhaps most important: Is your business creating agitation or bringing you joy and supporting you stepping into your potential?

Simplifying Small Business Success in the 21st Century
Glossary:

Business Mission: This is the tactics of what you do on a regular basis to secure your Business's Vision. A good example of this would be: To educate your marketplace.

Business Purpose: This is *why* your business exists. It's why you open the doors in the morning. There's nothing sexy about this. It is a factual statement.

Business Vision: The is the picture you paint of how your business and your marketplace will look once you have been in business for 5 -10 years. It's also your personal motivator.

Competitive Advantage: Strategies and aligning tactics to elevate the small business's position in its marketplace.

Entrepreneur: Person who starts a business.

Entrepreneurial Epidemic: Entrepreneurs who are infatuated with being an entrepreneur but won't step into the primary role of responsibility and action for their small business's success.

Entrepreneurial Explosion: This century's entrepreneurial expansion since The Great Recession.

King or Queen of Cushion: One who builds cushion into their daily schedule.

Micro-Business: A small business which has between 1 - 9 employees.

Peacefulness: Mindset and aligned actions for one to experience more joy and contentment through self-leadership, self-management, and daily practices.

People: All the different roles of people who are directly and indirectly related to a small business, its objectives, and the business owner.

Power Moves: Actions which directly impact the success of a small business.

Productivity: Tools and techniques one can apply to be effective and efficient.

Professional Development: The learning process of becoming a professional and owner of an evolving small business.

Profit: The surplus of dollars after a small business completes their annual government filing.

Profitability: Strategies and tactics which create a favorable financial outcome for a small business.

Small Business Owner: Seriously committed and growth focused entrepreneur who will do what is appropriately necessary for business success.

Small Business: Officially defined by the Small Business Administration as a business with less than 500 employees. Most people consider this to be organizations with less than 150 employees.

Strategic Advantage: Plans which give the small business long-term advantage.

The 4 Performance Pillars of Small Business TM: The 4 areas of small business focus: Profitability, People, Productivity, and Peacefulness (see model in Introduction).

The Grand Experiment of America and Entrepreneurialism: America's immigrants who became The Founders of American Business and gained prosperity through their business.

Meet Brilliant Practicing Expert™ Maggie Mongan:

Master Business Coach & Strategist | CEO | Global Conference Speaker | Author | Influencer | Possibilitarian

Master Business Coach & Strategist Maggie Mongan serves the small business sector. With over 30 years of business management and leadership, she became a Business Coach before Coaching became an industry! Maggie's figured out a unique and successful blend of traditional best practices and cutting-edge techniques to guide her personal and professional success. Her unwavering commitment to high performance and excellence undeniably delivers unconventional results.

Maggie's world is anything but average. She married a U.S. Marine in the 80s, raised two sons who excel in their respective music careers, is a Harley Rider, star gazer, and brings dreams to reality.

MAGGIE'S SPECIAL INVITATION FOR YOU:

Get access to a Free 30-day trial to Simplify Small Business Success Membership Site:
https://Academy.BrilliantBreakthroughs.com/

Business: Brilliant Breakthroughs, Inc.

Brilliant Breakthroughs, Inc. was established to support Small Business Owners in learning how to optimize, not maximize, their leadership and business performance. Maggie's background includes leadership and serial entrepreneurship via leading a non-profit and women's tech start-up, Certified Youth Ministry, and approximately a decade as the nation's go-to for manufacturing change-agents. She applies the practical wisdom of her Master of Management Degree, leadership experience, and psychology background into business models for her and her clients' businesses. Maggie swiftly helps Small Business Owners simplify their small business success by simplifying strategies and aligning actions to build their profitable and peaceful business.

Website: https://BrilliantBreakthroughs.com

Connect with Maggie on these social accounts:

LinkedIn: https://www.linkedin.com/in/MaggieMongan

Twitter: https://twitter.com/BrilliantBlogr

Facebook: https://www.facebook.com/BrilliantBreakthroughsInc/

Google+: https://plus.google.com/+BrilliantbreakthroughsInc

YouTube: https://www.youtube.com/c/brilliantbreakthroughsinc

Instagram: https://www.instagram.com/maggiemongan/

Mobile App for *Brilliant Breakthroughs for the Small Business Owner* book series:
Find us on your App Store as: **BrilliantBizBook**

Brilliant Breakthroughs for the Small Business Owner

Allow Me to Introduce Brilliant Practicing Expert™ Greg Nicholson by Maggie Mongan

Greg Nicholson is one of the most ethical men I've ever met – and he's a marketer! I mention this because many people don't believe marketing is ethical. It is and so is Greg. What intrigues me about his approach is Greg definitely knows how to influence and he does it in a practical fashion.

Greg and I were introduced to each other through good old-fashioned networking with a mutual friend. Yes, networking still works! Once we met, I was amazed at how Greg balances his caring heart with his no-nonsense marketing wit. Greg addresses a real need for small businesses – the need to be crystal clear when communicating their Market Dominating Position. He further discusses the indisputable value this provides businesses. He captured my attention. Why? Most small business owners don't spend enough time on this to better promote their business.

Greg has crafted a succinct teaching in his chapter to help small business owners look at the primary marketing message in a new light. He is gifted with taking rather large concepts and distilling them into a concise message for a consumer to understand, acknowledge value, and engage with the business.

If Your Marketing Efforts Aren't Bringing in New Clients, Here's the 3 Step Solution
by Greg Nicholson

Do any of these sound familiar?

- Your sales and business growth have plateaued
- You've tried different kinds of online and offline advertising and marketing, and nothing seems to work
- You're constantly worried where your next new client is coming from
- You're competing on price.

Then this chapter is for you!

If you're like many small business owners, you're looking for a sexy new marketing tactic, the next big thing, to get an edge on your competitors, and help you grow your business.

Well, I've got news for you. If the struggles above describe your situation, the reason isn't your marketing tactics, it's your marketing strategy. The difference between tactics and strategy is huge and it's vital you understand it.

Placing online ads, Social Media, SEO, PPC, sending out mailers, joining a networking group, attending trade shows, these are all TACTICS.

Many marketing tactics can be effective, if your marketing message is powerful and compelling. But that's the problem – the message is the STRATEGIC side of marketing – and yet, it's the most neglected.

Most fail to realize that the strategic side of the coin, what you say in your marketing and how you say it, is almost always more important than the marketing medium where you say it. If you fail to make this distinction, then you risk being unable to take advantage of certain forms of marketing and advertising which should be a part of your tactical plan.

"OK, so I need to focus on Strategic Marketing. What does this mean and where do I start?" Great question.

There are 3 main components of a predictable Client Generation System.

Client Generation System Components:

1. Ideal Client Profile
2. Market Dominating Position
3. The Conversion Equation

"A customer comes and goes. A client stays and continues to invest. It doesn't take that many clients to have a thriving business, but it takes a lot of customers." – James Arthur Ray, CEO Coach and NY Times Best Selling Author of "Harmonic Wealth"

Client Generation System Component 1: Ideal Client Profile

This is so fundamental; many small businesses gloss over this critical step. You must understand who your ideal clients are. How do you do that? The first step is realizing your ideal client is the person who shares your passion for your product or service. These are clients who want what you offer and are looking for a partner to help them solve a critical need of theirs.

Ideal clients are precious because they tend to stay with you a long time and buy multiple products and services. Client acquisition costs are real and often substantial, so it's good to remember that upselling and cross-selling to existing clients is MUCH cheaper (and easier) than acquiring new ones.

If you haven't done a recent phone interview of your best clients, whatever that means to you (i.e. higher purchases, more frequent purchases, repeat purchases), you really need to.

This is PURE GOLD INTEL and your best clients will be happy to spend 10 minutes on the phone with you. They'll share why they like doing business with you, why they choose you over alternatives, anything they don't like, recommendations for things you could provide or could improve, etc., JUST DO IT!

Your ideal client profile is more than just demographics like age, gender, income, education, etc., it's also psychographics – meaning what makes them tick? What are their aspirations, attitudes, and interests? Knowing this will be crucial for your marketing messages, as you aim to grab their attention by leveraging their emotional hot spots.

"You are 4 times more likely to upsell to existing clients than to sell to new clients." – James Arthur Ray

Client Generation System Component 2: Market Dominating Position

If your marketing isn't working, this is your #1 neglected piece of your marketing. Simply put, it's the reason(s) why clients buy from you instead of your competitors.

During an initial call with a client, a roofing company, I asked them what their Market Dominating Position (MDP) was. They answered stating how they use a certain polymer. I had no idea what this was and I advised them that very few of their prospects and clients did. Using a certain type of polymer may make them unique and perhaps, even superior than other roofing companies, but your MDP must be something your prospects and clients can understand, and most importantly, something your prospects and clients VALUE.

Let's bring this to your business. What, if anything, makes your business different from competitors, as perceived by your prospects and clients?

A Market Dominating Position is any value-added customer perceived benefit, or combination of benefits, which differentiates you from your competitors, and is strong enough to make your business the logical choice in the minds of your prospects and clients.

Prospects and clients don't buy based on price. They buy based on the VALUE they receive for the price they pay. This is why Nike and Starbucks can charge premium prices for their products, when other comparable options are available at a fraction of the price.

With this in mind, it's incumbent for small business owners to constantly look for ways to create added value. There are many ways to enhance how your business is perceived by your prospects and clients who want economical and efficient solutions.

WAYS TO ADD VALUE TO YOUR BUSINESS

A. Convenience

In our frantic, hectic world, nothing is valued more than our time. Save people time and effort and many will be happy to pay the premium.

Think Jiffy Lube. Let's face it - no one WANTS to get an oil change, but all car owners need them. So Jiffy Lube wins by offering a service people need and making it as convenient as possible.

Here are some categories of convenience: Location, Availability (days/hours you're open), Easier Ordering Process, Delivery, Payment Terms, Additional Services. So many options here, get creative and MAKE YOUR BUSINESS DIFFERENT and easy for a client to engage with you.

Jiffy Lube shines with convenient locations and hours, easy ordering process, and they have additional services like replacing headlight bulbs. Are there cheaper places to get your oil changed? Yes, but it's a bigger hassle and more time consuming.

My preferred auto repair shop washes my car when I get it serviced. By providing this added value service, they increase their chances of keeping me as a long-term customer. After all, I can't usually see the service they did, but I can tell that my car looks nicer and I drive away with a good feeling. Again, this is VALUE I can understand.

How can you leverage convenience as part of your product or service?

B. Speed

Speed and convenience go hand in hand. Are there ways you can get your products or services done faster than your competitors? If so, you've got yourself a market dominating position.

C. Training

Most of us are overwhelmed with everything we must do and keep track of. Many of the products and services we buy might be easy for the experts, but not for the everyday person. One of the areas where small businesses can outshine big businesses is by personal attention, including training to help your clients get the most benefit out of your products and services. If what you sell requires some technical expertise, even if it's minimal, including training as a value-add is powerful.

D. Remove Purchase Risk

Money-back guarantees and generous return policies are music to the ears of your clients. If your competitors aren't offering a money-back guarantee, you can make your business the only logical choice by doing this. Yes, it's a calculated risk to offer guarantees and returns, but unless there's something seriously defective about your products or services, you will make significantly more revenue with this policy than not.

HOW TO CREATE A MARKET DOMINATING POSITION

We've explored different ways to add value to your business. Below we'll discuss how you take the value-add and translate it into a Market Dominating Position.

Step 1: Determine your strategic position in the market.
What specific niche should your business focus on? Determine what unmet needs of ideal clients that your business could fill. For Jiffy Lube, it's fast oil changes for busy people.

Step 2: Determine your primary market dominating position.
This is the most dominating advantage. This separates you from your competitors. For Domino's, it was a promise to deliver a pizza in 30 minutes, or less, or your pizza was free.

Step 3: Determine your supporting business model.
How will you deliver on your strategic position and primary market dominating position? Jiffy Lube's are conveniently located, open early to late, 7 days a week.

Step 4: Determine your secondary market dominating position.
What additional competitive advantages does your business offer that your clients perceive as being different from your competitors? For Domino's it could be special pricing, broader selection of toppings or additional menu items.

Step 5: Create your market dominating position statement.
Combine steps 1-4 and turn this into your elevator pitch that differentiates you from your competitors.

Jiffy Lube Example: "Jiffy Lube provides busy customers with fast, convenient oil changes and refills your washer fluid, washes your windows, vacuums the interior, and checks your brakes in about 10 minutes, without an appointment, all for a flat rate."

Domino's Example: "Domino's provides busy customers with fresh hot pizza and other food items within 30 minutes or less. Our assorted pizza offerings combined with our value pricing makes Domino's affordable to everyone."

What is your market dominating position? Don't gloss over this step! This is THE reason why new clients will buy from you and it must be leveraged in all your marketing efforts.

Otherwise, you're stuck in a "me too" situation where prospects can't tell the difference between you and your competitors and they're forced to decide on price (race to the bottom) or who has the biggest name ($$$ on marketing). Either way, small businesses lose, as they typically don't have the margins to beat everyone on price nor the marketing budget to repeatedly get their name in front of everyone and their dog.

CLIENT GENERATION SYSTEM COMPONENT 3: THE CONVERSATION EQUATION

This is another critical element for successful Client Generation. Only a handful of marketing people understand this equation and those who do, can deliver incredible results.

Before we dive into this topic, it's important to understand if your product or service is a "considered purchase", meaning it's something your prospects think about for some time before purchasing. If so, there's a good chance you're missing out on serving 97%+ of your ideal clients.

How? Only 1-3% of your ideal clients are ready to buy at any given time. Note: These numbers haven't changed in over a decade of research.

The sales cycle typically goes through the following phases: First, your ideal client wants to engage in fact-finding, trying to figure out IF they want to buy what you offer (Future Buyers). Then, they move onto HOW to make a smart buying decision (Soon to Buy Buyers). Finally, WHO to buy from (Now Buyers). Depending on what you sell, a sales cycle could last a few days to a few months, maybe even longer.

If your marketing isn't working, you're likely failing to help your ideal clients:

1.   Make the best decision possible about your product or service

2.   Understand the advantages (value) of specifically buying from you

Most likely, all your marketing and offers only speak to Now Buyers, with things like "buy now and get a discount", "call now", "free estimate", etc. Let's get real here - NONE of these offers appeal to people who need to think about IF they should buy from you – remember, that's 97%+ of your market!

After all, a discount or free estimate is meaningless to someone who isn't yet sure they want your product or service (Future Buyers) or how to best make a buying decision (Soon to Buy Buyers).

Additionally, many businesses use messaging full of meaningless platitudes ("we're the best...", "we've been in business since..."), which is about YOU. Make sure your messaging is about the Ideal Client and what THEY WANT AND NEED, not you.

Seriously, if my back is killing me, I don't care where you went to school, how long you've been in business, your hobbies, or a photo of your adorable pet...CAN YOU SOLVE MY ISSUE OR NOT? That's all I care about and that's all your prospective clients care about too.

Fortunately, the Conversion Equation takes this into account so let's dig into this.

I.E.E.O.

Interrupt - Get qualified prospects to pay attention to your marketing. Accomplished by identifying and hitting your prospects' hot buttons. The interrupt is the headline that highlights a specific problem that your prospects are looking to solve.

Engage - Once your prospect is interrupted, it's critical to assure them that information is forthcoming and it will help them make the best buying decision possible. In other words, it must help facilitate their decision to pick you over anyone else. This is the job of your sub-headline.

Educate - Once you've interrupted and engaged your prospect, provide information which allows them to logically understand how and why you can solve their problem. When we educate, we need to reveal to your prospects the important and relevant information they need to know when making a good decision, and that your business – and yours alone – provides it to them. The interrupt and engage hit their emotional hot buttons. Educate is the logic they need to justify picking up the phone and calling you.

Offer - Provide prospects with a low-risk way to take the next step in the buying process. Put more information in their hands and allow them to feel in total control of the decision. Your offer will allow your prospect to feel secure in buying from you.

RESULTS REVEALED:

A psychotherapist in the Midwest - We clearly defined his Ideal Client Profile, crafted his Market Dominating Position, and leveraged the Conversion Equation on his website. After 45 days, he doubled the number of monthly inquiries from 30 to 60, which also doubled his client base, without increasing the amount he spent on advertising.

Many small businesses get caught in the endless cycle of churn and burn. Remember: how you sustain and grow a business is by providing value to your clients. At the end of the day, it's a value exchange. When you know who your IDEAL CLIENT really is, create a MARKET DOMINATING POSITION that capitalizes on VALUE they want. Then leverage the Conversion Equation. Once you do this you've truly set your business apart and massive growth is on its way!

"Forget about the money... focus on providing tremendous value to your clients with a methodical system, and your business will thrive." – James Arthur Ray

If Your Marketing Efforts Aren't Bringing in New Clients, Here's the 3 Step Solution
Glossary:

Client: A person or organization using the services or products of a professional person or company, such as an attorney. Client implies more of a relationship than a "Customer", which is more transactional.

Client Acquisition Cost: The total cost of acquiring a new client.

Client Generation System: A systematized and repeatable methodology to predictably attract and land new clients.

Considered Purchase: Purchases which are typically researched and considered carefully before making a final purchasing decision, such as buying a car. In contrast, impulse purchases are typically made on-the-spot, such as buying a pizza.

Conversion Equation: A 4-step equation that creates maximum response from Ideal Clients.

Cross-Sell: Sell a different product or service to an existing client.

Customer: A person or organization that buys products from a store or business on a transactional basis. Implies little or no relationship, such as a gas station.

Ideal Client Profile: A detailed understanding of who your best clients are, however you define that (i.e. large single purchase, multiple purchases that add up).

Market Dominating Position (MDP): Similar to Unique Selling Proposition, this is the defining reason(s) why your ideal clients buy from you vs. your competition.

Marketing Medium: Also known as marketing channel, it is where your marketing runs. i.e. Radio, TV, Print.

Now Buyers: Prospects who are ready to purchase today.

PPC: Pay Per Click. A business model whereby a company that has placed an advertisement on a website pays a sum of money to the host website when a user clicks on to the advertisement.

Psychographics: The study and classification of people according to their attitudes, aspirations, and other psychological criteria.

Sales Cycle: The amount of time between a first exposure to your offer and when the client purchases, and all steps in-between.

SEO: Search Engine Optimization. The process of maximizing the number of visitors to a particular website by ensuring that the site appears high on the list of results returned by a search engine such as Google.

Social Media: Websites and applications that enable users to create and share content or to participate in social networking such as Facebook, Twitter, and LinkedIn.

Strategic Marketing: What and how your marketing message is said in your tactical marketing.

Tactical Marketing: Where your marketing messages are said, such as email or print.

Upsell: Sell a more expensive product or service, or additional products or services to a client.

Meet Brilliant Practicing Expert™ Greg Nicholson:

Founder - Elevate Business

Greg Nicholson has closed over $63 million in online advertising technology and software sales with tech startups as well as Fortune 100 companies like Microsoft and Oracle. He was a leading member of the sales team at FrontBridge technology, acquired by Microsoft for over $300 million. He's currently the founder of Elevate Business, which helps small businesses grow their client base.

GREG'S SPECIAL INVITATION FOR YOU:

Book a complimentary Marketing Strategy Call with Greg Nicholson:
www.Elevate-Business.com

Business: Elevate Business

Elevate Business helps small businesses dramatically grow their business by 3X, 5X, and even 10X, by building a proven Client Generation System inside their business.

Website: www.Elevate-Business.com

Connect with Greg on these social accounts:

Facebook: www.facebook.com/Elevate.Business.1
Twitter: https://twitter.com/gregnmusic

Mobile App for *Brilliant Breakthroughs for the Small Business Owner* book series:

Find us on your App Store as: **BrilliantBizBook**

Brilliant Breakthroughs for the Small Business Owner

Allow Me to Introduce Brilliant Practicing Expert™ Dave Wallace by Maggie Mongan

Dave Wallace is one of the more interesting people I've met in a long time. He is a consummate professional and down to earth. It's hard to find that perfect mix of being practical and humorous, but Dave delivers it! His approach to life is filled with truly living life to its fullest.

With an extra-ordinary gift for detail and a memory to recall details in the moment, Dave is a great asset to everyone who engages with him. Simply stated, Dave adds value. When he decides to engage with something or someone, he's all in. His commitment level to achievement is unwavering.

Dave has the rare gift of combining strategy and tactics. It's not often we find someone who can see the big picture and then effectively drill down to the details of tactics; yet, Dave repeatedly does this. He is accurate when he talks about sales being anything but an activity of solitude. Dave knows the psychology, process, actions, and analytics, which deliver a favorable sales process. His sharp mind and keen eye serves his clients well as he helps them optimize their sales process.

Sales Suck in Solitude
by Dave Wallace

To the uninitiated, cycling looks like a very solitary activity. You carry your own water, food, spare tires, and maybe a CO_2 cartridge and pump. Many people feel the same way about sales – you're on an island. You have to figure out things for yourself and the old adage "If it's meant to be it's up to me" seems true.

Let me share a story that draws some interesting parallels: Here I am (see Figure 3) at the start of the 2016 Trek 100 - a charity bike ride to raise money in the fight against childhood cancer and blood diseases. A worthwhile cause. I'm smiling. The day is full of promise of a great ride through the farmlands of SE Wisconsin. That's how many of us feel when we approach another day at work. We're alert, alive, enthusiastic, and ready to attack whatever the day brings. We know our products, we know our services, we know (at least we think we know) what our customer needs, and we know we deliver tremendous value, at least in our eyes.

Figure 3.

Dave Wallace: Pre-ride 2016 Trek 100

Source: Courtesy of Dave Wallace.

Here's the first question:

Do you really know what your customer wants? As a matter of fact, can you easily identify your ideal customer?

It's like entering a bike ride and all you know about the course is what you see on a flat map. The route goes here, turns there, goes back over there, and finally ends. Without doing your research, how do you know what to expect? Are there hills? Is the road smooth? Are there rest stops where you can refuel and refresh? How busy are the roads along the route?

When it comes to your customers, or potential customers, do you know how they operate? Their philosophy? Do you know their buying process? Do you know who the key decision makers are? Do you know the real value your solution delivers to your customers so you can use that information when talking to prospects? No, I mean do you REALLY know?

The reality is most sellers can't definitively identify their ideal customer. They *kinda* know the value their customers get from their solution. However, rarely do they have any metrics to help potential customers understand the value they can realize by doing business together.

So, how do you get this information, whether entering a bike event or in the business world? You can, of course, do it all yourself. For a bike event, you can drive the course, noting the hills, rough road patches, where the traffic is fast, and possible rest stop locations. Or you can lean on others. Someone has mapped the course, selected the rest stops, has a topographical map of the route, and all that information is available to you for the asking.

When it comes to business, you can leverage the power of data. You can go online and likely find mountains of information about your potential customer. You can ask/interview colleagues. You can - gasp - even interview existing customers to understand, truly understand, the value they got/or are getting from doing business with you.

Back to the question - do you know what your customer wants and do you even know what your ideal customer looks like? Simon Sinek goes a bit farther and says, "most companies have no clue why their customers are their customers" (2009, p. 16). Did you know that as much as 85% of opportunities in your sales forecast will never close? Why? There are many reasons:

- The buyer doesn't understand the value of your solution

- The seller isn't speaking to the right person - someone who can decide to move forward even without a budget

- The buying organization has conflicting agendas and can't make a decision.

Bottom line: if you don't understand your customer you'll spend valuable time pursuing opportunities that will never close.

How does this relate to cycling and my Trek 100? I had to answer similar questions:

- Was my bike ride ready?

- Did I understand the course?

- Did I understand the environmental effects on the ride - was it going to be hot (yes!), humid (yes!), a headwind as we headed for home (yes!)?

- Were my riding partners in agreement as to how we were going to handle our ride?

Before I went on the ride I had my bike tuned up. I reviewed the course. I located the rest stops. I knew where the hills were. Based on the weather forecast, I knew we needed a plan to hydrate and keep cool (more on that later). Our group developed a plan to make sure we helped each other out, shared the workload, and kept each other *in the game*.

Whether getting ready for a bike ride or trying to make sure your sales pipeline is filled with the right prospects, you can, and should, leverage experts. Bike mechanics keep your bike in tiptop shape ensuring each pedal stroke transmits power to propel you forward.

Business experts can help you understand and quantify the value your solution delivers, create case studies and other metrics to help you deliver compelling stories. Doing so ensures all your sales energy is transmitted toward those prospects who will actually buy from you. You can, of course do it alone, but why?

Next question:

Can you quantify the value your solution delivers?

In keeping with our comparison, let's talk about the value of your *training* solution for a bike ride. If every time you ride, you go on the same course and at the same speed, you'll become a marginally stronger rider. But the riders who really improve, get value from their training, are the ones who vary their training. They do intervals, do hill repeats, go for long rides – you get the idea. Their training solution delivers significant value. It's the difference between finishing that hot and humid 100-mile ride or getting a ride home in the support van at mile 57. Not fun.

When we talk about the value a business solution delivers, it must be about what your solution does for the customer. When asked what value they bring to their customers, most business leaders will articulate what they do. Rarely will they describe value. Why? Mainly because they haven't asked their customers.

This seems shocking - but it's painfully true. We're so happy we made the sale. We don't want to jeopardize any future business by asking if our customer actually achieved the outcomes they documented when they built their business case to do business with us.

How do you quantify the value? You talk to your customer! What? Yes indeed, you actually talk to your customer. "Your existing customers are a veritable fountain of information regarding the business value of your product or service" (Konrath, 2006, p. 65).

Find someone who thinks strategically, who thinks about the economic impact your product or solution has on their organization. Did they save money? Generate revenue? Mitigate risk? Much like your coach can analyze your training routine, your customer will help you understand the value you deliver.

Sales and cycling – solitude sucks in both cases.

Now that you have your ideal customer/know your route and you can quantify the value you deliver/have trained in a way that is valuable, what next? Armed with that information you start making logical predictions.

In cycling, you can predict if you are really ready for the challenging ride ahead of you. And you might even be able to predict, within reasonable parameters, when you will finish. In business, you can start predicting the value your future clients get from doing business with you (Koser, 2009, p. 109).

Why is this so important? Because it sets you apart from your competition. They are all talking about what their product does and how cool it is - hard to believe that's still the case today, but sadly, it is. You, on the other hand, are talking about value. You're talking the language of business. "If you can't articulate a business case to a buyer, you haven't earned the right to ask for the business" (Jeff Koser, CEO, personal communication, July 18, 2017).

Last question:

Sometimes, despite the best planning, things go wrong. What then?

First, my cycling story. I successfully finished the 100 miles. By doing so, I met all the expectations of the people who supported me and donated to the MACC Fund. Yet, here I am (see Figure 4) about an hour after the ride ended.

Figure 4.

Dave Wallace: Post-ride 2016 Trek 100

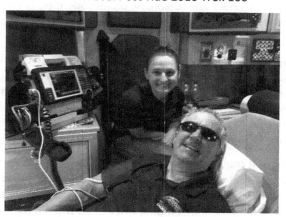

Source: Courtesy of Dave Wallace.

As you can see, I'm not with my buddies enjoying a cold drink and sharing the day's adventures. I'm in an ambulance, hooked up to several monitors, with an IV drip (not in the picture). While I'm smiling here, I'm pretty sure I'm still somewhat delirious. Yep, you guessed it, I didn't follow my plan, didn't listen to my buddies, and ended up in a bad situation.

We've all been in a similar position. Maybe we didn't end up in an ambulance, but we've had sales opportunities, which we thought were rock solid, end up on life support. Some we rescued, some we didn't.

Most, if not all, of these situations could have been avoided if we 1) had a solid plan, 2) worked our plan, 3) had the situational awareness to recognize when things were going off track, and 4) leveraged colleagues and experts to help us get things back on track.

How does that happen?

On the bike ride, I got cocky. I was feeling good, despite the heat and humidity. My buddies were going slower than me, so I figured they were the ones struggling.

While I was thirsty, I wasn't drinking a lot. While I was tired, it didn't occur to me that it was due to more than just a long day on my bike. I wasn't situationally aware and I didn't follow my plan. I didn't pay the ultimate price, but I did have a good scare, not to mention how my riding partner freaked out when I passed out as we departed the venue!

In business, we get a good vibe from our customer and we stop following our process. They give us early "buying signals" and we think, "I've got this, I don't need to follow my process, just ask for the order." Or, we know in our gut that we need to engage more people to get the necessary buy-in for the solution. After all, while there may be one person who signs off on the project, the days of someone saying "yes" when his or her subordinates/colleagues aren't on board are over.

Research shows there are almost seven different buyers, or buying influences, in any complex business-to-business sale (Dixon, Adamson, Spenner, & Toman, 2011, p. 7). Getting over confident, thinking we can bypass key elements in our process is just asking for trouble.

Let's wrap up. My goal in telling my cycling story is to illustrate that when you look at someone riding a bike your tendency is to think of that person as a solo performer. Those of you who ride a lot, or race, know that's so far from the truth it's laughable. In sales, sometimes we make the same mistake. We think it's all about us (cue the laugh track). If we can just get in front of a client we can make the sale. We have, after all, "the gift of gab." Sorry boys and girls, it's 2017 and it's a whole new world.

Sales is a team sport. It requires a team of experts working together to develop a plan which allows the organization the greatest chance of success. This means working together to understand your ideal customer, the value your solution delivers to the customer - in their words, not yours - and understanding what to do when things get off track. As you know, there is much more to sales than these three steps. But these are foundational. Without them, all the rest is like trying to ride a bike with two flat tires.

Sales Suck in Solitude
Glossary:

Biking Terms

CO2 Cartridge: A small metal container, about the size of your thumb, that holds highly pressurized CO_2 (carbon dioxide) gas. Together with a special release valve, they can inflate a standard bike tire in seconds.

Intervals: Training in which an athlete alternates between two activities, typically requiring involving efforts of very hard exertion followed by an easy effort (the interval). These are repeated any number of times, or until exhaustion.

Rest Stop: A location, usually staffed by volunteers, that provides the cyclists with food, drinks, bathrooms, maybe a bike mechanic, and lots of encouragement.

Topographical Profile: A map that shows the elevation changes of an area, especially helpful in understand where the big hills are so a cyclist can manage their energy output

Business Terms

Buying Process: The process that sellers must go through to actually sell something to a company. Can be complex with many steps, or very simple.

Metrics: A quantifiable measure that is used to track and assess the status of a specific business process.

Sales Forecast: A listing of a company's current sales opportunities including, at a minimum, the date the opportunity was listed, the expected revenue, and the expected close date.

Solution Value: The value the customer expects to get from their purchase of products and services from someone. It can be measured over time, and should always be the based on what the customer expects, not what the seller expects.

Internal Business Justification: Buyers build a business case for making a purchase. The enumerate the expected value the purchase will bring to their company

Prediction of Value: Selling organizations that understand the value their past customers have received from their product or solution can, with a bit of research, begin to predict the value a future customer can expect.

Buying Signals: Physical or verbal cues that a prospect or customer sends that indicate interest.

Meet Brilliant Practicing Expert™ Dave Wallace:

Founder | Principal

David Wallace has over 40 years experience in all aspects of business development, from being an individual contributor to leading a team. He's also a student of sales. He understands sales is not about how much he knows about his products and services, it's about helping his customers solve their problems and achieve their goals. A proud graduate of the University of Notre Dame, David has been married over 35 years, has two children, one grandchild, and an English Setter. He is an avid cyclist and current heads up Ride MKE, a cycling club with more than 300 members.

DAVE'S SPECIAL INVITATION FOR YOU:

For a complementary prediction of value, click bit.ly/bayridgepov

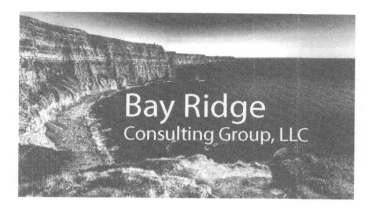

Business: Bay Ridge Consulting Group, LLC

Business to Business sales is more complex than ever. Small businesses that understand who their ideal customer is and focus their energy on only those customers will increase their average sale size, decrease the length of their sales cycle, and increase their pipeline close rate. Translation: they increase revenue. Using proven processes and methods, along with 40 years' experience in business development, Bay Ridge Consulting Group helps small businesses improve their sales effectiveness and efficiency so they can find, close, serve, retain, and expand their ideal customers. We help your sales team become sales superstars.

Website: https://www.bayridgeconsultinggroup.com/

Connect with Dave on these social accounts:

Personal LinkedIn: https://www.linkedin.com/in/davelwallace

Business LinkedIn: https://www.linkedin.com/company-beta/15223052/

Mobile App for *Brilliant Breakthroughs for the Small Business Owner* book series:
Find us on your App Store as: **BrilliantBizBook**

**Performance
Pillar 2**

PEOPLE

Brilliant Breakthroughs for the Small Business Owner

Allow Me to Introduce Brilliant Practicing Expert™
Stacy Kaat by Maggie Mongan

Stacy Kaat is a firecracker of a person who cares deeply about others. Her keen eye is essential for great photography; however, she also applies this to all areas of life. Stacy's game is one of authentic beauty. She is a fun-loving person, who has phenomenal depth, and sees the world differently – as it truly appears.

When working with Stacy, she seeks until she finds the essence of her client. Her process begins even before you step into her studio. She guides you through steps to help you understand your essence and what you want to convey through your images. Stacy helps you remove your masks and creates a safe space for your truth to be revealed. Then, the photographer takes over to work with you to achieve your goal.

Stacy's approach dignifies her clients through what many consider is an unnatural process. When you book a session with her, you get a different outcome than most photographers can provide. Why? Stacy guides you through a learning process of how to utilize your headshot for professional development, while she assists you in creating your ideal headshot for optimal attraction.

Why Your Headshot May be a Turn-off and How to Turn It On!
by Stacy Kaat

Don't chase away your target market with a bad headshot! People are looking for you and your product or service. Don't miss the opportunity to connect with potential customers using your headshot is an effective marketing tool. With guidance you can attract more customers than ever before!

Katrina Cravy, Motivational Speaker and Media Coach, who spent 24 years as a television consumer reporter, states, "Your headshot is so important, the first thing the media is going to do is take your name and 'Google' it. They're going to want to see, 'What does this person look like?' and 'What is their overall brand?' We've had people that have pitched us as a Life Coach, and we've gone to their LinkedIn page and it's a guy with a woman hanging around his neck at a bar. They don't get the gig. You are basically saying 'No' to business by not reviewing what you are putting out online visually" (personal communication, June 6, 2017).

Since people want to know, like, and trust you before they will consider doing business with you, hire you for a job, or go on a date with you, chances are very high they will *Google* you. Do you know what their search will find? The first thing they will see, when they click on a link with your name, is your headshot. And people will form an opinion about you based on this first impression. You either have a chance at getting the gig or you don't!

According to Psycologicalscience.org, it takes less than 6 seconds to form a judgment about you based on your appearance. This should scare you! In those few seconds of judgment, you either turn people off or turn people on.

I know, the word judgment has a bad rap, but it's a primal self-preservation instinct to make judgment. It's a technique to protect us from possible danger. If your headshot poses no danger, it doesn't mean people will be turned-on by it. Your appearance must also resonate with them in some way. People need to *feel* something emotionally when they look at your headshot.

Humans are naturally social. Often, we respond and react to people throughout the day without even realizing it. We use our personalities, along with our appearance to form first impressions. We naturally build our first impression while speaking, smiling, making eye contact, and building rapport.

When we meet people in person we are usually turned-on or turned-off by their personality! It's their personality that makes us like them or not, and appearance is not quite as critical. Online, appearance is the first thing we see – it speaks volumes about you.

Your appearance infers whether you're reserved or creative, serious or fun, messy or neat, or just plain run of the mill. Even though who we are on the inside is most important, what we show on the outside is what people see. It's in our best interest to give them our best headshot, share a bit of our inside, maybe even turn them on to us - encouraging them to want to know more!

Active, successful business owners devote significant time online, posting and commenting on social media. Each of these interactions is an impression for people to visualize when they think about you. Positive or negative, each impression helps them form an opinion of you.

Each time we post, our headshot and our name are there to remind people who we are and what we look like. With all this visibility, we need to be aware of the message our headshot is sending, and build a business personality to represent ourself well. Robert Grede, best-selling author of *Naked Marketing-The Bare Essentials* [Prentice Hall] says, "It's helpful to be memorable, but not in a negative way" (personal communication, June, 13, 2017).

People judge with their eyes. It's how we choose what we like to wear, how we decorate our homes, what flowers we like, who we date or become friends with, and even what we eat. Choices can be based on past experiences, personal taste, marketing, and what we have been exposed to visually and otherwise. We eat, shop, and buy with our eyes. Furthermore, much of what we buy is based on our first impression.

The good news is that we have the power to create a favorable first impression. Nothing like using the viewer's perceptions to our advantage! Your headshot, and other photographs of you, is a great way to take full advantage of the visual nature of the human brain. People are looking for you. It's up to you to give them the first impression they want to see. If you do this well, they will be encouraged and want to know more about you!

Sarah Crowley, Personal Stylist, Owner of FaD Consulting, LLC, and author of *Feel Beauty Full: 7 Steps to Allowing Natural Beauty* says, "People don't see their own beauty... People like people that are comfortable in their own skin." Sarah is right, when we are comfortable with knowing who we are, we can embrace our imperfections and our personality comes out more naturally in photographs (personal communication, June 8, 2017).

As a photographer, I can't tell you how many times I heard, "I don't look good in pictures," or "I hate getting my picture taken". People fear they won't look natural or like themselves. I believe the biggest underlying problem is fear of being judged by our looks alone. We are extremely self-conscious about the details of our physical bodies. Unfortunately, we don't see our true beauty and the value we offer the world.

A great headshot may not look like what we envision. Michael Cavotta, a Headshot Photographer and Personal Branding Coach known for bringing people face-to-face with their authentic selves, will set you straight. Michael says, "No one is as hung-up on your imperfections than you. Your headshot is about how it makes other people feel, not what you actually look like" (personal communication, June 12, 2017). Well said, after all we are not our audience.

I hired Michael Cavotta to photograph me. Before the photo shoot, I mentioned how uncomfortable I felt because I had gained a few pounds. After the shoot we never discussed the details of what I looked like. We chose the photograph that best represented my personality. The goal was to give the viewer a glimpse of my authenticity - a *feeling* about who I am.

Headshot fears and concerns are legitimate. What turns people off, what turns people on, and how to find a photographer who understands how to work with Headshot Fears will help alleviate your fears. A professional photographer who can infuse your personality and message into a headshot will create a memorable first impression that turns people on to you.

Don't turn off people by making the following mistakes.

HEADSHOT TURN-OFFS:

1. No profile picture. Having a headshot is better than no headshot.

2. A dark or blurry headshot. A crystal clear photograph demonstrates you care and are professional.

3. The Selfie. Selfies are obvious and will not be taken seriously in the business world.

4. Too much skin. Provocative clothing has been shown to prevent job promotion. But, if you're selling something sexy, it can work for you if it fits your brand. Don't do this unless it is entirely appropriate.

5. Outdated looking hair and clothing. Update your hair and clothing to show you are updated in business.

6. Picture that includes more than your head and shoulders.

7. Lack of personality. Your headshot should be expressive of who you are.

8. Too much distraction. Bright clothing, lots of jewelry, or background clutter will distract people from seeing your face.

9. You don't look like you! If you have updated your hairstyle, glasses, or it's been more than two years since you had a professional headshot, it's time for an updated photograph.

10. A glamour shot. According to photofeeler.com, using a glamour headshot for a business profile picture will produce a different perception about you than when it is used as a dating profile headshot.

How to create an effective headshot and memorable first impression:

Debra Pyne, Professional Hair Stylist, states "You want to present yourself in an inviting way. I think people should not be afraid to let their inner *you* show - your essence. You should be groomed. Have your hair and makeup done by a professional. You want to be polished - it's an investment" (personal communication, June 11, 2017).

Brynn Doering, Professional Hair and Makeup Artist for film and photography, states, "You don't need to look 10 years younger in your photo. You don't want something so dramatically different [for your headshot], that when you show up, [in person] the people you're meeting don't know who you are. Look real and approachable, you don't want to look like a cardboard cutout" (personal communication, June 13, 2017).

While appearance is important for online first impressions, we shouldn't let our insecurities dictate how our picture should look and feel for others. Appreciating our inner self and our strengths is what gives us our true beauty and authenticity. When we see and accept this fact, we can express ourselves confidently in pictures and in our messaging, and leave the fears behind!

HEADSHOT TURN-ONS:

1. Your headshot is a crystal clear, well-lit picture that shows your eyes and enhances your natural great looks.

2. Your clothing enhances your skin, brings out your eyes, creates a nice framework for your face, and shows that you are professional at whatever it is that you do.

3. You took the time to do your hair and makeup, and still look authentically "you".

4. You know who you are, and are not afraid to show it!

5. Your expression and overall style radiate your personality.

6. Your headshot is a close up of your head and shoulders.

7. Your headshot has a simple background, which does not distract from your face.

8. I see you at a networking event, and I recognize you right away because your headshot reveals your personality. YES!

Marketing expert, Robert Grede, reminds people that, "Your online profile – Facebook, LinkedIn, Instagram – is part of your resume. Any boss worth his or her salt will check out your online profile." If you are looking for a job, a promotion, new customers, or just trying to create credibility, you should be concerned about what people think about you when viewing your headshot (personal communication, June 13, 2017).

Your headshot is your first impression online. That initial touch point; those few seconds, are the most important time to connect with your viewer. If the viewer is turned-off by your headshot, chances are pretty good they will look no further to find out about you, your product, or your services. This is a sad moment for you, because you have now lost a potential business, client, job, date, or whatever it is you were hoping to gain by using your headshot.

If you hire the right professional photographer to create a headshot that turns on people, I'm certain it will create positive *feelings* for your viewer. Do I want to know more about you? Absolutely!

HOW TO HIRE THE RIGHT PHOTOGRAPHER:

Choose a photographer who specializes in headshots. Look at their testimonials and headshot photographs to see if they resonate with what you've learned in this chapter. When you talk to the photographer, it is your job to communicate how you will be using your headshot.

The photographer should be asking a lot of questions to get to know you. You should feel confident the photographer will deliver the headshot you both agree is right for your business. Not all headshot photographers are the alike. Choose carefully, someone inexpensive or new probably will not have the experience or skills necessary to create your desired results.

An effective headshot represents you authentically, projects what you want people to know about you, and is aligned with your message. A great headshot will help you build your business personality with confidence.

REMEMBER:

- Everywhere you are online, social media, LinkedIn, Meetup, etc. your profile headshot has the potential to repel or attract. It will do so in less than 6 seconds.

- Portray yourself as confident, smart, funny, or whatever elements of your personality you want to emulate to help attract the right people to you.

- Your headshot must be authentic. If you portray yourself as someone you are not, it won't take long for people to figure out who you are based on your behavior and messaging.

- The right headshot is an investment and gives your business personality a layer of trust and appeal.

- Post the same headshot everywhere to enhance recognize ability, become memorable and credible in the eyes and minds of others.

- Choose a photographer who will help you create the right headshot, bringing out your personality, and helping you attract the right people.

After reading this chapter I think you know why your headshot may not be what you had envisioned. It's probably not the best reflection of you. Now, you may be concerned how others will perceive what you have put out there for your first impression. Scrutinizing what image you are projecting is essential.

WARNING:

Do not get hung up on this being all about you. It isn't. It's all about how you make the viewer *feel*. I hope you can put any insecurities you may have behind you. Then, envision your headshot as an effective tool to move you forward in your personal and professional life. Cheers to Building YOUR Business Personality with Confidence!

Why Your Headshot May be a Turn-off and How to Turn It On!
Glossary:

Business Personality: The visual and verbal representation of a person online and in person.

Cardboard Cutout: A headshot that looks like everyone else with no personality.

First Impression: The few seconds when someone views a headshot online and forms an opinion based on what they see.

Google you: When someone types your name into the Google search engine to see what websites have information about you.

Headshot: A photograph of a person's head and shoulders.

Headshot Turn-offs: Common mistakes people make with their headshot that can leave a bad first impression.

Headshot Turn-ons: Ways in which you can create and utilize your headshot to give the viewer a positive first impression.

Know, Like, Trust: These words are used together in business as information that a person or company provides about themselves that can help people get to know, like and trust them to provide the product, service, or relationship they are seeking.

Personality: who a person is, how they behave, and what value they offer.

Posting and Commenting: What you post on social media.

Professional Photographer: A person who derives 100% of their income from photography and continually grows their photography skills.

Profile Picture: Photograph of a person used on social media websites.

Selfie: A headshot that one takes of oneself, usually with a mobile phone.

Social Media: Websites that enable users to create and share information, ideas, and messages with other users.

Meet Brilliant Practicing Expert™ Stacy Kaat:

Photographer

When I was a teenager, fashion and advertising images shaped my idea of how people should look. Unfortunately, those images don't represent who we really are and what we have to offer the world. Over time, I learned who we are, our beliefs, and our strengths are what makes us unique. Yet, we are judged by how we look. What we project in our photographs affects how people perceive us. I'm excited when I can collaborate with people to infuse their business with personality and create authentic pictures, so they can present themselves professionally with confidence.

STACY'S SPECIAL INVITATION FOR YOU:

Turn YOUR Headshot On today!
http://www.stacykaat.com/contact-stacy

PHOTOGRAPHER

Business: Stacy Kaat Photography

Photographer Stacy Kaat believes in the power to create headshots that utilize the visual nature of the human brain to attract the right people. Anyone can take a picture, but Stacy examines the subtleties of facial expression and lights the face to bring out the unique qualities of each individual. She has a gift of making people feel comfortable, providing an environment that allows people to relax and be authentic to who they are. Stacy helps dynamic people infuse personality into business pictures so they can attract the right people and communicate what it feels like to work with them.

Website: http://www.stacykaat.com

Connect with Stacy on these social accounts:

LinkedIn: https://www.linkedin.com/in/stacykaatphotography

Twitter: https://twitter.com/StacyKaatPhoto

Facebook: https://www.facebook.com/stacykaatphotography/

Google+: https://plus.google.com/u/0/+StacyKaat

Instagram: https://www.instagram.com/stacykaatphotography/

Mobile App for *Brilliant Breakthroughs for the Small Business Owner* book series:

Find us on your App Store as: **BrilliantBizBook**

Brilliant Breakthroughs for the Small Business Owner

Allow Me to Introduce Brilliant Practicing Expert™ Mike Raber by Maggie Mongan

In every sense, Mike Raber is a true gentleman. Mike's skills and capabilities of leadership, building relationships, and action may be overlooked by those who don't know him well. Don't be fooled by his subtle approach of care and concern when you engage with this master, for he has it all under control.

Mike has lived boldly in some extreme situations, which has assisted him in refining his approach to people and success. Some of Mike's experiences are filled with shocking and learning moments. He's all too happy to share snippets of his personal and professional journeys – especially learning to optimize Eastern and Western philosophies and practices for better living.

Perhaps even more amazing is how Mike has applied these to building an impressive and strong professional network through his unique relationship building techniques. I think it's safe to say, "Mike knows people." He also knows how to make great connections. Additionally, he offers a bonus of having an insurance background, which can help you effectively secure the business you've taken time to birth and grow. You'll be glad you took time to meet Mike.

How to Avoid the 3 Most Common Challenges
Every Small Business Owner Encounters
by Mike Raber

All great businesses begin as an idea or passion waiting to be transformed into physical form. You may have a dream, passion, or an idea for a great business; yet, when it comes to building a small business, it's very important to have a solid core foundation built on marketing, organizational development, and financial in place to support the needs of your business. Without these three core elements in place, small businesses will be challenged and eventually implode.

When it comes to starting a small business, or taking an existing business to the next level, there are three common challenges small- and mid-sized business face. It doesn't matter if the business sells widgets, or is a service related business. At the end of the day, the three core fundamental components are the same. As the saying goes "business is business." All small businesses must build and manage relationships, develop the business to sustain itself, and create a financial foundation to support the business.

FIRST COMMON SMALL BUSINESS CHALLENGE

The most common challenge small business owners face – not having a consistent marketing or lead generation system in place. Most small businesses are lacking consistent performance because lead generation for new business is not a priority. Without a systemized marketing approach a good business idea will perish.

All effective marketing programs incorporate certain key components which determine the level of effectiveness of the business's marketing program or campaign. For instance, campaigns must be carried out over a predetermined period of time. They must be relational in nature. Remember my quote, "People don't care how much you know until they know how much you care."

Your relationship building must be consistent, like a mailing that is sent out the first week of the month, each month over a long period of time, instead of quarterly or occasionally. Over time consistency builds trust. Additionally, your marketing must be consistent with a common theme, jingle, or campaign that keeps you in the forefront of your target market's mind on an ongoing basis.

Many small business owners have more of a transactional focus, rather than a relational focus. When I work with small- and mid-size business owners, I find they spend a majority of their time perfecting their craft. The plumber fixes toilets, the accountant crunches numbers, and the real estate agent shows houses. They also spend a significant amount of time putting out fires, handling customer service, and administration activities. Only at this point does lead generation finally fit into the schedule.

Without leads or people on your calendar, your business will dissolve. In business and sales lead generation is undeniably one of the most important and simultaneously overlooked business activities. It often gets the least amount of attention – right up there with business and financial planning.

As with many businesses, if marketing or lead generation is addressed, often it is misdirected. The primary focus shifts to lower cost forms of advertising and other forms of passive marketing. The focus should be about proactively going out and finding new leads. A common approach is to begin attending networking chamber lunches or other community based social and business gatherings.

Examples of passive approaches are advertising, direct mail, and hoping for referrals (but not actively working a referral system). Proactive lead generation examples are cold calling, knocking on doors, networking, or actively working a referral system. Additionally, "It's also very helpful to have a video presence, especially when it comes to social media. What do you want your video to accomplish for your business to succeed?" (David Kocol, Videographer, personal communication June 13, 2017).

Your goal should be to sit down with potential prospects or advocates and constantly focus on building strong relationships with existing clients or customers. The objective should be to continually add these new contacts into a relational database consisting of past and present clients, new contacts, and leads who properly fit your business. The trick to a well-run marketing program is to have it as systemized and automated as possible, without losing the personal touch.

The growth of your business is dependent upon a strong systematized database built upon relationships, not just a mailing list. I notice many small business owners will often spend a large amount of money and time trying to acquire leads to fill their pipeline. Unfortunately, once they get busy they neglect the very activities and people who initially brought business in the door. This neglect creates peaks and valleys in the day-to-day operations of the business and revenue.

Probably one of the most over looked ways to generate leads is through networking. Networking is a contact sport. It takes work to turn a contact into a lead. Business owners will attend a networking event in hopes of finding new business or contacts. Yet will often fail to have a desired outcome before they get there. This is a big mistake.

An example might be a financial advisor thinking, "I'm going to the event tonight and will meet three people between the ages of 45 and 60 who have at least $100,000 to invest." Or, "I'm going to set three appointments with people who want me to help them prepare a financial plan." If you know your ideal outcome, you will know what types of questions to ask when talking with people.

Many people will go to an event and try to get as many cards as possible, or they may just pick out a couple people and talk to them the entire time. In these cases, they could leave without making any actual contacts at all. Conversely, other people leave networking events with multiple new contacts or may have set appointments before they leave the event.

The most important key to networking is to ask people questions. In negotiation, there is a saying: *The person who talks first loses!* In networking, the same holds true. The next time you're at a networking event, try to learn four to seven new things about each person you speak with specifically regarding his or her business.

When it comes to business cards, I have found there are two common mistakes people make at networking events. Some will treat their business cards like they're made of gold and hesitate to give them out. There is also the person who pushes their cards into the hand of anyone who has a hand. Warning: Don't let this be you! Being selective with handing out your cards is always an effective approach.

Whenever I go to a networking event or meeting, before I even enter the room, I think, "Why am I here and what is my desired outcome? What type of client am I looking for? How many appointments do I want to make?" Upon entering, I first scan the room and see if there is anyone who immediately matches the criteria for my goals. Then I move around the room and ask people questions that will aid me in determining if they match those requirements.

Don't just go to events to find your business's new leads or clients. Instead, think of the needs of other people you know. Share which businesses would best fit their specific need. Additionally, seek people whose businesses would complement what you're doing. Find your *power partners*. A power partner is someone or a business who is a perfect fit for your business. An example would be a real estate agent meeting a lender or a personal trainer meeting a nutritionist.

When talking with someone at a networking event, ask yourself the following questions: "Do I know anyone this person may be able to help?" "Does this person have a need that I can service?" "Would this person make a great advocate for my business?" "Could this person become a good power partner?" Try to limit conversations to a few minutes. This way, if there isn't a good fit, you can politely excuse yourself and move to the next person. If there is a fit, then try to set an appointment for a later time.

Tip: When booking the appointment, only give a few times of availability to meet; otherwise you'll give the impression that you're not in demand.

Once you're in the appointment, ask open-ended questions. Some examples of open-ended questions are, "How long have you been an accountant?" or, "What is your ideal client like?" Then spend as much time as possible learning about the other person and what they do. Continue to listen for their wants or needs. Last, send a personal note expressing how you enjoyed talking with them and how you look forward to learning more about what they do.

SECOND COMMON SMALL BUSINESS CHALLENGE

The second challenge many small business owners face – not paying enough attention to the organizational development of your own business. Do you have a defined value proposition? Why is your business or idea any different from others in the market place? Why should people do business with you? It's very important to have a personalized business plan that is designed around your goals both for your business and your life.

The working business plan shouldn't be any more than four pages, ideally shorter and should discuss why you're in business. It should state: (1) what is it that sets you apart, (2) what you should be doing each day in your business, and (3) goals' dates. Don't get so caught up in the day-to-day tasks that you eventually stray away from your overarching plan. I often suggest our clients to daily review their working business plan – or minimally at the start of each week.

Do you have a solo versus team mindset? "By ourselves we can do great things; yet, together we can climb the highest mountains" – Mike Raber (2015). Too often small business owners try to do everything themselves and become a *Jack of all trades, master of none*. Regularly, I notice small business owners trying to become competent in many different areas. Ultimately, they end up not doing very well in any of them and their business flounders.

Another pit many small business owners fall into, is they spend the bulk of their time working on less important activities, which could be delegated or outsourced. Thus, they are not focusing on the more important or core activities needed to effectively run their business. True champions focus on what they do best and surround themselves with others whose strengths are their weaknesses.

As your small business grows, it's important to develop a team of outside advisors or mentors to network with and have as a resource to assist with more complex projects. True, you may be in business for yourself, but you should never be entirely by yourself. Even in today's high-tech world of endless reach, successful business requires strong foundational systems and the support of a community surrounding it.

New small business owners encounter a similar obstacle – not having enough tenure in business. For this reason alone, budding small business owners are primed for failure. Just because someone is very good at something or has the next big idea doesn't mean they should jump into business. There is a learning curve all small business owners must go through. It can become extremely expensive if they choose to learn these lessons on their own. Business success comes down to the commitment of consistent planning and supporting actions implemented into your business. As Ben Franklin stated in the 1700s, "If you fail to plan, you are planning to fail." Financial and business planning is not just action—it is a mindset, as well.

THIRD COMMON SMALL BUSINESS CHALLENGE

The third and probably the largest challenge business owners face – inconsistent business or financial planning. When it comes to building a strong financial foundation under your business, there are six key areas of importance.

6 Financial Keys for Small Business Owners

Financial Key 1: Consistent cash flow management

Without consistent positive cash flow, your business will run like a three-legged stool with one leg broken. It may appear sturdy until a need arises.

Financial Key 2: Create an emergency fund in place for your business

Ideally a healthy business should have between six months to one year of operating expenses set aside for the day when an unexpected need occurs. I have noticed that if a business doesn't have an emergency fund in place, it seems like both business and life will become a string of emergencies.

Financial Key 3: Proper protection of the business

Often small business owners will treat insurance as that ugly expense they would rather leave under the carpet. Many businesses I have worked with don't have enough insurance on place – leaving their business vulnerable to potential risks. Conversely, others were paying too much on insurance for certain assets, liabilities, etc. It's essential for a small business owner to review their insurance at least once a year.

Financial Key 4: Debt reduction

Acquiring debt can be a powerful way to add an asset into the business. It allows a business to earn more while leveraging cash flow. Yet if not watched carefully, debt can quickly wrap its tentacles around the business and choke it out of existence. If properly managed, debt can be a good tool for growing a business. If poorly managed, it will be the death of even the strongest business.

Financial Key 5: Develop short-, mid-, and long-term investment

Granted, the first and most important area of investing for your business is reinvesting back into the business so it will continue to grow. However, just like your personal life, it's important for the business to diversify its earnings outside of the business in-order to help strengthen the long-term objectives of the business.

Financial Key 6: Consistent succession plan development for the business

When some small business owners decide to retire, they simply turn out the lights and sell whatever assets their business may possess. Unfortunately, they never realize the true enterprise value their business should have created for them personally.

"Most people think time/financial freedom means they can do anything they want, but I've redefined time/financial freedom to mean I don't have to do what I don't want to do" (Amber Chang, Cofounder, personal communication, June 8, 2017). As you grow your business, it is essential to continually monitor and grow its true enterprise value.

WRAP-UP

Today, most people wouldn't drive in a foreign city without getting a map or directions. Then why do they allow their most valuable resources to exist without developing a financial roadmap? Wouldn't it make more sense to be guided to their preferred destination?

I often tell clients that if they continue to manage their money and businesses the same way they did last year, their finances and business will look the same next year. If that is acceptable to them, that's great. However, if you want more, you need to change what you are doing today. In other words, are you on or off track to reach your business or financial goals to make your dreams come true?

How to Avoid the 3 Most Common Challenges
Every Small Business Owner Encounters
Glossary:

Advocate: Someone who believes in your mission and takes personal interest in helping you grow your business through referring people to you or offering support.

Campaign: A specific, defined series of activities used in marketing a new or changed product or service.

Cash Flow: The total amount of money being transferred into and out of a business, especially as affecting liquidity.

Contact Sport: A sport in which the participants necessarily come into bodily contact with one another.

Debt Reduction: Debt relief or debt cancellation is the partial or total forgiveness of debt, or the slowing or stopping of debt growth, owed by individuals, corporations, or nations.

Enterprise Value: Is a measure of a company's total value, often used as a more comprehensive alternative to equity market capitalization.

Financial Planning: Looking at one's financial cash inflow and outflow currently and into the future. It's planning both during the accumulation and the distribution phase.

Lead Generation: The action or process of identifying and cultivating potential customers for a business's products or services.

Listening for Wants and Needs: Being able to listen to and accurately interpret a customer's needs and repeat it back to the customer so as to qualify it with what you think they want.

Networking: An effective low-cost marketing method for developing sales opportunities and contacts, based on referrals and introductions – either face-to-face at meetings or gatherings.

Open-ended Question: Question designed to encourage a full, meaningful answer using the subject's own knowledge and/or feelings. It is the opposite of a closed-ended question, which encourages a short or single-word answer.

Organizational Development: A field of research, theory, and practice dedicated to expanding the knowledge and effectiveness of people to accomplish more successful organizational change and performance.

Passive Marketing: Passively waiting for the phone to ring or for business to come to you with no effort.

Power Partner: Someone or a business that is a perfect fit for you're business. An example would be a real estate agent meeting a lender, or a personal trainer meting a nutritionist.

Prospects: Someone (be it a person, a department in a company, or a whole company) who has an interest in your business or your product.

Re-investing: The best way to build wealth. If you're a business owner, reinvesting is crucial to your company's continued growth and success. It's putting income or revenue from the business back into the business so it can grow.

Succession Plan: The process of designing a business for it to be sold at a later point for a predetermined value.

Value Proposition: Explanation for prospects to learn why they should do business with you rather than your competitors. Defines the benefits of your products or services.

Meet Brilliant Practicing Expert™ Mike Raber:

Wealth & Business Coach

Mike in a business, wealth coach, author, and speaker. He has spent the last 35 years working in, starting, building and managing various businesses. He has a wide range of experience in business, real estate, and financial education. He has worked with many professionals and small business owners helping them grow their businesses, while continuing to serve their clients at a deep level.

Mike is very passionate about helping small business owners design a business and financial foundation develop to help them reach financial independence, and determine what's truly important to them, empowering them to live their life with a purpose.

MIKE'S SPECIAL INVITATION FOR YOU:

Dream so big that you will need a team!
Go to www.microbizcorp.com to join us or learn more.

Micro Business Corporation

Business: Micro Business Corporation

Welcome to the Micro Business Corporation. We are a membership based community comprised of a powerful group of professionals, entrepreneurs, and small business owners. We provide a proactive systematized lead generation system, key business/wealth planning solutions, and a powerful network of like-minded professionals and business owners, working together to help each other succeed in a supportive and dynamic environment. We believe that alone we can do great things, yet together we can climb the highest mountain. It's our goal to serve as the cornerstone between our members and the people that have a need for their products and services.

Website: http://www.microbizcorp.com/

Connect with Mike on this social account:

LinkedIn: https://www.linkedin.com/in/mikeraber

Mobile App for *Brilliant Breakthroughs for the Small Business Owner* book series:

Find us on your App Store as: **BrilliantBizBook**

Brilliant Breakthroughs for the Small Business Owner

Allow Me to Introduce Brilliant Practicing Expert™ Jake Nawrocki by Maggie Mongan

Unstoppable is the first word that comes to mind when I think of Jake Nawrocki. Jake's zest for living life is undeniable. He is practical, caring, and wants everyone to accomplish their goals.

What makes Jake unique? He knows how to take a stand with conviction, and he doesn't do so haphazardly. Perhaps that's the fireman in him. This capability allows Jake to make good things happen. He embraces the concept of being *raw,* or genuine. Many people are attracted to Jake and his message because he is authentic and speaks with enthusiasm.

Jake is a leader who knows how to step forward into adversity and coaches others to do the same. He holds an annual event where attendees are empowered to do a fire walk. I want to say, "Pay attention to where Jake Nawrocki is going because he's on fire." Yet, I do realize this may not be the best way to convey he's a rising star who cares about the success of others. He believes everyone's message is important and we're all teachers to one another. Jake is committed to helping small business owners share their unique message through the power of podcasting.

Your Voice ON AIR
by Jake Nawrocki

Would your business look different if you had your own radio show? Would listeners think of you as an authority in your business, would you create a deeper connection with your customers, and as a result would more people buy your products or service? I hope you said *yes* because radio is powerful. Unfortunately, as a small business owner, chances are you don't have deep pockets or the connections to get a time slot on open air.

Lucky for you technology now allows small business owners the opportunity to create an online radio show to reach billions of online listeners. This new kind of radio is called podcasting. Podcasting is hitting the online marketplace by storm!

Podcasting allows anyone with a microphone, computer or tablet, and Internet, the ability to start and operate their own online radio show. Celebrities, publications, influencers, government agencies, media outlets, and small business owners like yourself are starting a podcast because it's changing how we connect, build relationships, and impact others.

Podcasting shows are basically on demand content. Any listener can turn your show on whenever or wherever they want. Listeners don't need to have an internet connection to tune in. Most importantly, your voice, your message, and your business goes with them anywhere they go. Most, if not all, smartphones come preloaded with a podcast playing app. Today's new vehicles have a podcasting app right on the main entertainment screen now. This means that all ages are tuning into podcasts, not just young techie kids.

Have you heard of red ocean versus a blue ocean from *Blue Ocean Strategy* by Kim & Maubourgne (2005)? The concept is simple: Stop competing in the overcrowded red water and get into the blue ocean to have your business thrive. The red ocean I am referring to is traditional marketing. We can agree that everything you do as a small business owner is marketing. Anything from creating a website, blog posts, making videos, social media posts, sending coupons, handing out flyers, and paying to sponsor events, are all great but competition fierce and so is the price.

If you want to compete in the red ocean of the online space you have your hands full. Facts MarketingProfs reveals that each day over 2.73 million blog posts are published (2015). According to Fast Company magazine (2015) over 300 hours of video content is uploaded t YouTube every minute. Now consider incalculable number of social media posts shared. Each day, this is your competition.

Most people are shocked when I share with business owners that the only blue ocean currently existing is podcasting. I say this because the amount of the shows in the game is undeniably small. At the time of this publication, there are only 600,000 podcasts on iTunes.

In 2013 Apple made a big deal posting they just reached over 1 billion listeners subscribed to podcasts. FYI: iTunes is not the only player in the podcasting space but it's the biggest with the best credibility. There are other podcast directories, such as SoundCloud and Stitcher Radio, who have big audiences for you to impact with your show. Let me repeat -

only 600,000 shows for an audience over a billion people. I think it's is a great place to hang your shingle.

Starting a podcast is not just for online small business. It can be a storefront for business too. Posting a podcast to iTunes has major search engine optimization potential. If your ideal customer searched for keywords relating to your business, and you owned a podcast, on the first page of results this would display: http://itunes.apple.us/podcast/your-business-name-here. Would this help you attract your customer?

Having your business associated with Apple indicates to your customer you're legit, you're the authority, and you're awesome. Okay, being awesome might be over the top but the truth is you're hanging in the blue ocean with Apple next to your business name. I can attest to this statement because having a show on iTunes was the sole reason I landed a $3,000 speaking contract.

In early 2013, I decided to start a business on personal development. I wanted to become a big-time speaker like Tony Robbins - quite the lofty goal, I know. I decided online was the place to be, so I created a website and started blogging. As I learned more on how to gain a larger audience, I started to compete in the red ocean of online marketing. As the months went by, I was gaining some traction but not much was happening with my business. My big turning point was when my wife told me that we were going to be expecting our first child. I felt pressure to push the accelerator on my business and jump into a blue ocean I knew nothing about.

At the time, I was a fan of podcasting. When I would walk dog, Yogi, my headphones would go in. Podcasts allowed me to gain knowledge, wisdom, and over time build a deep relationship with the host. Each host I listened to had a unique style, entertainment value, and their personality showed through their voice. One host who I really connected with is, Pat Flynn. Pat Flynn has a great podcast and business called *Smart Passive Income*. During one show, he was telling the audience how podcasting changed his business and suggested all business owners should start. It wasn't until he said the following that I realized I should start my own:

"Podcasting is one of the most intimate connections you can make with an audience. There is no other platform where a person will put your voice inside of their eardrum and listen from start to finish."

I started to laugh, but he nailed it. If a friend or family member was talking close to me, I would back away. But I could listen to Pat for hours. That was the moment when I decided to jump into the blue ocean and start a show. I launched my show. It's a moment you never forget because you are sending your voice, personality, and passion for your business directly to people who need and want your information.

Since my show has been aired, it has been downloaded over 4.7 million times from listeners in 78 different countries. Having a show allowed me to get on stages, network and interview influencers and experts, sell more books, products, and services, and create an impact on someone's life. I don't say this to impress you but to impress upon you that the same possibilities can and will happen for you if you start a show.

Before you start stapling sound dampening foam to your ceilings, I want to remind you that podcasting is a commitment. The good thing for you is you're already committed! You made the conscious decision to start a business. If you choose to swallow the podcasting pill, you must give your podcast time, energy, and your full raw self. Let me repeat, you must give your full raw self.

Your raw self is who you really are – imperfections and all. I am talking to you, the person who doesn't know all the answers, the person who sometimes stutters when you get locked on a thought, and the person who talks with a few *umms* and *ahhs* during conversations. If you can bring your raw self – entailing your own personality, stories, and perspectives to your podcast, listeners will love you and want more of you.

New podcasters make the common mistake of trying to be someone they are not. It's a unique experience talking into a microphone. You need to remember to be your raw self. If you act like someone else, your audience will be gone forever. Even if you're raw every episode, some people simply won't like your approach, style, or you being you. You can't control that!

My show has eight one-star reviews. If you read the reviews, some are nasty, but I have 194 five-star reviews that are awesome. If you live in the land of being raw, you can't be mad at the nasty messages. You are who you are: voice, personality, and value in all.

Your voice provides all the senses of your business in audio format. There are no other distractions between the listener and the host; that's why you need to be consistent with your online voice. What you say, how you say it, and the energy you put into it will allow you to have a successful show. Many shows lose traction when all they do is sell their products or service to a nonconnected audience. Remember to sell your raw self to the audience. When you do this well, they are willing to take the step to learn what you offer.

At the end of the day, you're trying to drum up sales, exposure, and strengthen your business. Any effective business owner understands business success is not based solely on how much money it makes, rather it's about building relationships. The more relationships you have, the more your customers will do the selling for you.

Marketing expert, Shiv Singh (2012), says it best, "The purpose of a business is to create a customer who creates customers." Your voice has the ability to create relationships, your voice will connect, your voice is the driving force of your business. Use your website or physical location to sell your products. Use your podcast to build the relationship to drive listeners into your online or physical store.

Over the course of the last four years, I have learned a lot and helped new podcast shows launch. In the following I answer a few frequent asked questions (FAQs) you may have regarding podcasting.

FAQ 1: There are current, popular shows that talk about my exact same type of business. Is there room for me?

Yes, the more podcasts talking about the same type of business is a great thing. It shows many people are interested in the business you own and operate. There are ways to differentiate your show compared to the current ones. If you're a woman talking about health tips, you can direct your show to only help women instead of talking about men and women like other shows.

Even if your show shares the exact same content, you're the difference maker. You have different experiences, viewpoints, stories, and a different personality to attract and connect with a listener. This is what makes podcasting so unique. Communicating with your voice has so much more power than other mediums.

FAQ 2: If I am putting all this energy and time into creating a podcast show, what else can I do with the recordings?

Once you record your show, you can hire someone to transcribe your episodes. You can find people on UpWork.com or Fiverr.com to economically transcribe for you. Once you have the transcription, you can turn it into a blog post or chop it up and deliver chunks of content in your social media.

If you have a few podcast episodes, you can turn it into an eBook. You can either sell the eBook or give it as a free lead magnet in exchange for an email address. You can also take your *audio only* episodes and upload it on YouTube and Facebook for additional exposure. If your episodes answer customer questions, you can email it to a customer looking for additional details. There are endless possibilities. Be creative to see how your content can best serve your customer.

FAQ 3: Starting a weekly show sounds exciting, but I feel I don't have enough content to keep the show going long term, any suggestions?

You're not alone. This is a fear for most podcasters. A majority of shows today are interview based for this reason. For example, if you're a health coach, you can interview authors, exercise experts, nutrition experts, professional athletes, or spiritual health experts. Having an interview-based podcast is beneficial for both the podcaster and guest. It's a win for you because you get great content for free, and your interviewee gets to reach out to your audience.

There is no shortage of possible people to interview. If you see this as an option for your show, all you need is Skype and a plugin called Skype Recorder. Skype Recorder will record the audio or video of the interview and all you do is put that conversation into your recording software. Additionally, this is beneficial for you because it allows you to expand your networking within your niche. The more experts you talk with, the more others will see you as the expert.

FAQ 4: I don't have the time to host a weekly or daily podcast, should I still start one?

YES, you should! There are two podcast formats available. First: if you are strapped for time, I would suggest to just upload content about your business and let it sit there. This next approach is more suited for a structured business such as a carpet cleaning business. As the owner, you could release 10 episodes all at one time and just let it sit there. Each episode uploaded could talk about one must-do maintenance tip to keep your carpet looking fresh. This provides value to the listener and creates search engine optimization for your business. A helpful tip assures you place a call to action at the end of the episode. This will take the listener into a funnel of free info or for coupons.

FAQ 5: What type of equipment do I need?

You need three pieces of equipment: a microphone, recording software, and somewhere to upload the MP3 file to iTunes. First, don't get caught up on online forms reading page after page of microphone reviews. If you want to be serious about posting without taking out a loan, purchase the Audio-Technica ATR2100-USB microphone. It will cost $70.00, the quality is very good. I personally used this microphone for my first 60 episodes on my show. It also connects to your computer via USB, so it can plug into a Mac or PC without any issues.

Second, you need software to record your voice from the microphone to computer. If you're a Mac user, I would use Garageband. It's already preloaded on your computer and easy to use. If you're a PC person, download a free software called Audacity.

Third, you need to upload your audio file so it can get sent to iTunes and other online podcasting sites. Without getting all geeky, look up a company called Libsyn.com. It's what I and 90% of all other podcasts use. Libsyn.com will charge you monthly fee ranging from $5-$75.

As a business owner, there's a variety of ways to get your business in front of new customers. This chapter may excite you or scare you. Podcasting is an effective tool to reach an untapped market. Stop telling yourself "podcasting won't work for my business" because your competitor is reading this and saying this is exactly what is needed for their business. Here's to your success!

Your Voice ON AIR
Glossary:

Audacity: Free, open source, cross-platform audio software for multi-track recording and editing.

ECAMM: A service that records audio or video of a Skype call conversation.

Fiverr.com: An online marketplace offering tasks and services, beginning at a cost of $5 per job performed. This site is primarily used by freelancers who use Fiverr to offer services to customers worldwide.

Garageband: An audio recording software that works perfectly with Mac computers.

Libsyn.com: Provides everything your podcast needs: publishing tools, media hosting and delivery, RSS for iTunes, a Web Site, Stats, and Advertising Programs.

Podcast Play App: An application that can be placed on a smartphone or computer that plays podcast shows.

Skype: An instant messaging app that provides online text message and video and audio chat services.

Smart Passive Income: A company started by owner Pat Flynn. Pat Flynn teaches others how to create income online.

SoundCloud: A Social sound platform where anyone can listen to or create sounds and share them everywhere.

Stitcher Radio: A website that allows you to upload podcasts or to listen to podcasts.

Syndicated: Publish or broadcast (material) simultaneously through a number of platforms.

Upwork.com: Global freelancing platform where businesses and independent professionals connect and collaborate remotely.

Meet Brilliant Practicing Expert™ Jake Nawrocki:

Podcaster | Founder | Coach

Jake Nawrocki is the founder of Operation Self Reset, a brand that teaches individuals and teams to create breakthrough results. Jake has reached over 4.7 million people with his top-rated podcast and high-impact presentations. Each year Jake hosts live events and mastermind groups to help individuals reach their next level.

Jake resides in Milwaukee, WI with his wife and three sons, where he works full time in his community as a Lieutenant for Milwaukee Fire Department. What sets Jake apart is his unique ability to juggle and balance his family, work, small business, and Real Estate properties.

JAKE'S SPECIAL INVITATION FOR YOU:

Free video will share five podcasting secrets to increase sales, clients, & increase exposure: http://operationselfreset.com/

Business: Operation Self Reset

I teach small businesses to create a podcast to generate more sales, build a larger audience, and to create extreme credibility online.

Website: http://operationselfreset.com/

Connect with Jake on these social accounts:

LinkedIn: https://www.linkedin.com/in/jakenawrocki/

Twitter: https://twitter.com/jakenawrocki

Facebook: facebook.com/osrfanpage

YouTube: http://www.youtube.com/c/JacobOperationSelfReset

Instagram: https://www.instagram.com/jakenawrocki/

itunes: https://itunes.apple.com/us/podcast/operation-self-reset-self-help-101-confidence-self/id648755583?mt=2

Mobile App for *Brilliant Breakthroughs for the Small Business Owner* book series:
Find us on your App Store as: **BrilliantBizBook**

**Performance
Pillar 3**

PRODUCTIVITY

Brilliant Breakthroughs for the Small Business Owner

Allow Me to Introduce Brilliant Practicing Expert™ Nancy Lucchesi by Maggie Mongan

Once upon a time, there was a little girl who was filled with curiosity. She explored life and people. One day she found herself in the middle of life – raising children, excelling in her career, and pondering the bigger picture.

Sometimes she was resilient, and other times not. She would dream of different ways of being. One day she decided to emerge and began living her dreams. She carved new paths for herself. Even though these new paths had some scenic detours, she stayed true to her vision and steadied her course. Guided by fate, fortitude, and a few more plot twists, she reached her next milestone and smiled. Her name, is Nancy Lucchesi. Repeatedly, she's dreamed and achieved.

Nancy has a very strong technical aptitude. She knows how to translate dreams into reality. Nancy's gift is help you develop and manifest your dream of business growth and success via technology. I hear many Small Business Owners express how they can't afford a mobile app. I know there is another path. With conviction Nancy states, "Not so! Dream – it is possible to get what you want, the way you want, and economically."

Unleash Your Mind, Unleash Your Growth!
by Nancy Lucchesi

What is an entrepreneur? Have you really asked yourself this simple question?

Entrepreneurship is a burning desire to bring to life a vision. Most entrepreneurs are not motivated by profit but by a measurement of success only they have set themselves. Most of the time, it's about a feeling of fulfillment and growth. As I grew up, I never gave thought to becoming an entrepreneur, yet here I am.

How did I become an entrepreneur? While working for another small business, I found myself feeling I lacked something in my life. Day after day, I showed up to work, did the same mundane tasks, and returned home, all to help someone else bring their vision to life. It did not satisfy me, jazz me, or fuel the burning desire I held to have more in my life. I was not living my purpose.

One day, a client and I spoke about an opportunity with a local business. I researched it, studied and worked with the company for a while. After about a year, they decided to make a shift and the Mobile App division was open for me to acquire and spin off on my own. The next thing I knew, I became the founder of my own business. By becoming an entrepreneur, I found the path which led me to live my purpose. I feel fulfilled and jazzed to get up every morning, ready to embrace the world.

But it was not just not a simple transition. I made several mistakes in my journey. I fell into the habit of thinking by doing busy work, I was being productive. I learned many things and mostly, I needed to change my thought pattern. It came to me one day. Conventional thinking did not serve me. I wanted my business to have a unique impact to help other businesses bring their vision to life. I found by just changing my thoughts, which led to empowering my actions, my business exploded.

To truly bring a passion to life, it must be fueled by an enormous 'Why?'. Your Big Why, when defined at its core, will make you get up every day to do what you do with more passion and drive than you ever imagined. What's your Big Why? Have you ever asked yourself? Have you ever defined it?

My Big Why is to give all small businesses the opportunity to compete in the mobile market with the big money corporations with a Mobile App to showcase their business. This country was built on entrepreneurs with a vision. We are all connected on some level. I want to help them expand their vision. When I see people use a Mobile app for one of my clients, it jazzes me. I know my client is bringing their vision to life. It gets me up in the morning and keeps me going late into the evening.

You've defined your *Big Why*, now what? Next you must retool your thoughts around your goals. Everyone in business tells you to be successful, you must set goals. On top of it, the *experts*, and I use the term loosely, state they must be obtainable and reasonable. Plus, experts state goals are to be set on past performance. I'm here to tell you there's a better way. The past does not equal the future. It's all well and good if you want to just obtain some obscure level and call it an achievement. But to truly breathe life into your vision, you must change your thoughts and clearly state your intention.

Picture a board room prepared for a shareholders meeting. Encircling the elegant walnut football shaped table are twelve high-back maroon leather chairs lined with brass rivets. In the center of the table lays a mirror tray holding a crystal cut vase displaying fresh flowers flanked by two sweating ice water pitchers. Memo pads, pens, and filled water glasses are carefully placed at each seat. The laptop is prepped to project the PowerPoint presentation with the latest figures on the screen covering the wall.

The board members file in sporting their finely pressed suites, crisp white shirts, perfectly knotted ties and neatly folded handkerchief peeking out their breast pockets. They each take their customary seats as the PowerPoint begins to play an introduction video as the theme from Rocky plays in the background. The CEO enters last, wearing a huge grin and carrying a box of cigars under his arm. He takes his seat at the head of the table and pushes his chair back to watch the video presentation.

"Gentlemen, we did it. We achieved all our goals." The group claps as they pat each other on the back. "Yes, we maintained our market share. We remained the same. Cigars all around."

Suddenly, the door opens, in walks a very non-descript woman. "What's your dream? What's your Big Why? What gets you up every morning to do what you do?" The room went silent.

Now shift your mind's eye to a small bakery, in a small town, next to a big city. The owner operator walks into the back room where he finds his wife. "Check this out, honey." He points to the paper in his hand. "We did it. We made the Bernstein wedding memorable. They loved the cake, especially the cake top. They sent us this fabulous thank you note."

Warmly she says, "How sweet, makes every day worth getting up. And guess what, we were named best bakery of the year again. Love it. I feel so abundant, fulfilled." He adds, "Me too. We made record numbers last year. I never imagined being so prosperous."

Suddenly, the door opens, in walks a very non-descript woman. She inquires, "What's your dream? What's your Big Why? What gets you up every morning to do what you do?"

"Why? Why do we do what we do?" he said without even thinking. "We are on a mission to bring sunshine to every person in the city. The simple things in life are the best." The why became a part of their every day.

"Our dream? To be the only bakery people seek to make every occasion a special memory" his wife chimed in. "Our Big Why gets us up in the morning to do what we do. We want to bring a little happiness to everyone. We strive to dazzle them with our charm and make them smile every day."

When you look at these two businesses, you might think the big boardroom is more successful than the small bakery. After all, they are the big boys, right? But are they more successful? The bakery embraced their vision, their dream, their Big Why. They lived their passion. The boardroom just made some arbitrary goal, based on past results. They congratulated themselves for just staying the same. They did not express or feel the passion of what they do every day. The bakery felt their purpose to their core. They knew they succeeded when they brought their vision and purpose to life. They experienced abundance every day in all levels of their life.

Goals allow you to feel accomplishment. Fine, but don't stop there. Change the term goal to dream. A goal lacks passion. Especially if it is task oriented. The pitfall with tasks is they can turn into busy work. A dream fuels passion. After all, Martin Luther King Jr. said, "I have a Dream" and great things happened. He did not say I have a goal.

Dreams are not just for kids. When you dream you dream big, you unleash your mind. You leave the constraints of your false limitations and your limiting beliefs behind. Don't allow your family and friends to limit you with their reality beliefs. Bring to life visions which you never thought possible, only dreamed of in your mind's eye. Open yourself to go beyond some random benchmark. Reach for the stars and embrace your journey. Change your thoughts from goals to dreams and watch them grow.

One of the biggest obstacles for small businesses when bringing their dreams to life is spending money on their business. Most look at the expenses as a means for keeping their business open. They get overwhelmed when they pay items like rent, utilities, and furniture. Each one is viewed as an expense, not an investment. They cut dollars because they 'can't afford' to allocate funds to grow their business. Things like advertising, technology, payroll and professional services are usually the first to go. They start to do all the little tasks themselves to keep expenses down and the hamster wheel effect begins.

Just a simple shift in your thoughts will open so many windows of opportunity. The easiest alteration to make is to change a few simple words. Change the word *expense* to *investment*. By investing in your business and, more so, yourself, your business will break free from the wheel and explore fresh territories.

Ask yourself this question every time you are presented with a financial decision. How will it get me closer to my dream? What is my Return on Investment, or ROI? More importantly, what will I lose by not making the investment? This can be done with every dollar you invest, no matter how large or small. For example, you pay rent, it's an investment. If you did not pay rent, you would not have a place for your customers to engage in your product or service. Instead of looking at this as an expense, think of it as an investment to bring your vision to life.

Even something so simple as eating lunch needs to be thought of as an investment. You are investing in your health and vitality so you may keep your business growing. Whether it's money or time, open your mind as you unleash it to view everything you do as an investment in you. Your business will flourish when you do.

Einstein's definition (1951) of insanity is "doing the same thing over and over again and expecting a different result." Every time I hear this phrase, I laugh because I see evidence of insanity every day. People keep repeating the same steps and thought patterns, expecting better results. Small simple changes bring huge growth. You don't have to shift everything at once. Small steps bring change. It's important to take an honest look at each shift to see if it has brought you closer to your vision.

Are you doing what you do best and hiring the rest? Most business owners feel they must do it all and get bogged down with tasks. In reality tasks need to be done by someone else. Yes, you need to have a complete understanding of every aspect of your business. After all, it is your business. It does not mean you must do it all yourself.

A wise person capitalizes on their individual strengths and knows when to allow others to do the same. Hiring does not mean just having an employee. Although proper effective employees are a real asset, you don't always have to bring people on payroll to achieve the same outcome.

One option which helped me, especially when first starting out, was to bring on interns. In exchange for an education, I received completed tasks and projects. I assigned them responsibilities which were not effectively using my time. Later, as your cashflow improves, consider contracting professionals for areas outside of your strengths. Experts in their field, can bring exceptional production leading to increased profit. After each project, always remember to analyze your ROI to make sure you have received value. If not, make changes. It may be easier to work with contractors than trying to mold an employee to be the expert.

In the book, *Three Feet from Gold: Turn Your Obstacles into Opportunities,* authors Lechter & Reid (2009) speak about seeking counsel and not advice. In short, they emphasize it is wise to turn to experts for guidance and counsel. Try not to seek and do not blindly listen to advice from family and friends. The majority of the time, your family and friends do not share your vision and certainly are not an expert in the area you need help.

If you have a legal question, seek an attorney. If you want to increase your sales, seek a business coach skilled in your area. If you need technology advancement, seek the services of a tech-savvy professional who is familiar with your industry. If you want to get your business noticed, seek an advertising specialist in the arena you wish to advertise. Do not ask your teenager to run your social media campaign. They may know how to use social media, but they don't know how to use it to grow your business. Always remember you are a professional in your field and want people to recognize your expertise. Hire support people, experts in their field to give you counsel. Doing so will grow your business and bring your vision to life.

Don't just haphazardly get into debt just to hire the best without a plan. Rather, invest your resources wisely after you have considered the value. If you must, take a loan to invest in your business. But do so sensibly. Ask yourself, "What will be my ROI? How will this enhance my business?" Be conservative, but not to a point of holding back your growth. Lean on experts to give you counsel to educate yourself.

Have a complete understanding of your financial books so when you work with an accountant you know your true financial picture. Understand advertising and social media. Know exactly how to do it and what impact it has on your business. Embrace technology and learn how to use it effectively in your business. Technology, when used properly, will bring a significant ROI.

Embrace every aspect of your business and know exactly how to do everything. Then and only then, define what you are good at and hire your weaknesses. Always evaluate your ROI, whether it be an investment of time or money. Maximize all your resources.

In the end, it is all about your business, your vision and your dream. Bob Proctor (1984) said, "If you can see it in your mind you can hold it in your hand." Be happy with where you are and excited to grow. Know your true Why. Your Big Why, when defined at its core, makes you get up every day to do what you do. Change your thoughts to align with your dreams. Seek counsel from experts who understand your field.

Always be open for change and innovative ideas to nurture your business. You chose to be an entrepreneur because something within you drives you to live your passion. Begin every day by setting your intention. Embrace it. Grow with your intention. Most of all, enjoy every moment actualizing your intention. Remember to step out of your comfort zone. I assure you, your dream will follow.

Unleash Your Mind, Unleash Your Growth!
Glossary:

Arbitrary: Based on random choice or personal whim, rather than any reason or system.

Big Why: Your passionate reason for doing something.

Dreams: A vision in your mind of something you wish to create.

Embrace: An act of holding something closely.

Empowering: To be given strength.

Entrepreneur: A person who starts their own business, no matter how big or small.

Founder: A person who establishes a business.

Goal: An arbitrary level of achievement set to measure success.

Hamster wheel: Doing the same thing over and over.

Limitations: A condition of limited ability; a defect or failing.

Mobile App: A marketing tool used to enhance and showcase a business to sell products or services.

Obstacles: A thing that blocks one's way or prevents or hinders progress.

Opportunity: The possibility of joining a business for a career.

Overwhelmed: Give too much time or thought to something; inundate.

Purpose: A person's sense of resolve or determination.

Success: A personal feeling of achievement.

Thought Pattern: Way of thinking.

Unleash: To open or set free.

Vision: An image in your mind about your future.

Meet Brilliant Practicing Expert™ Nancy Lucchesi:

Founder | Mobile App Expert

Founder of Unleashed Mobile Apps, Nancy Lucchesi's work centers around helping other small business owners bring their visions to life. After several decades of business experience, primarily in sales, Nancy finds joy and satisfaction in helping other business owners succeed. She considers small businesses the heart and soul of this country and believes they play a key role in strengthening local communities.

Nancy's favorite part of her work comes when her clients succeed in growing their businesses through mobile technology. Nancy is an avid Packers fan and loves to travel, especially when it leads her to a beach.

NANCY'S SPECIAL INVITATION FOR YOU:

Click Here to Unleash Your Business with a Mobile App:
http://unleashedmobileapps.com/

Business: Unleashed Mobile Apps

Wondering what a Mobile App can do for your business, think about this. Consumers spend more time on their mobile devices shopping, scheduling appointments, and looking for information than ever before. People use 2-4 apps daily to function in their daily lives. Unleashed Mobile Apps was founded with the small business in mind. We help small businesses compete with the larger corporations on the Mobile App platform. We help businesses with a loyal customer base easily stay in contact with them. Having a Mobile App for your business will save you time and money.

Website: http://unleashedmobileapps.com/

Connect with Nancy on these social accounts:

Personal LinkedIn: https://www.linkedin.com/in/nancylucchesi/

Business LinkedIn: https://www.linkedin.com/company-beta/22330488/

Personal Facebook: https://www.facebook.com/profile.php?id=100009031301636

Business Facebook: https://www.facebook.com/unleashedmobileapps

Twitter: https://twitter.com/UnleashedApps

Mobile App for *Brilliant Breakthroughs for the Small Business Owner* book series:
Find us on your App Store as: **BrilliantBizBook**

Brilliant Breakthroughs for the Small Business Owner

Allow Me to Introduce Brilliant Practicing Expert™
Dave Rebro by Maggie Mongan

I know many people believe it isn't possible for a techie to be a people person too. Well, what if they do exist? I'm here to introduce you to Dave Rebro, commonly known as The Tech Therapist. Dave serves humanity by helping us meld our professional and personal worlds with the digital world in a powerful manner.

It is unique for any professional to have deep listening skills. Dave's listening skills out-perform many helping professionals. His gift is he understands process. It doesn't matter if the process is workflows or our mental process, he understands the power of sequence and organization. His expertise supports him to mindfully move through a process, or from one to another, to gracefully accomplish end goals. A bonus of Dave's approach is he innately knows how to honor the emotional frustrations that emerge for clients as they learn new tools for tech and productivity improvements.

Dave's confidence in his tools, strategies, and tactics allows him the opportunity to be 100% present to his clients' needs and concerns. Admittedly, Dave is my preferred Tech Therapist. Why? He is helping me continually refine my personal and business's digitization to better support 21st century success.

Why Small Business Owners Don't Sleep at Night
by Dave Rebro

Do you ever lie awake at night thinking about your business? Have you tossed and turned in bed because you were worried about a project not being completed or by the amount of items on your to-do list? Ever struggle with trying to turn off your mind at night, but just couldn't?

As small business owners, entrepreneurs and solopreneurs, we wear many hats and have many responsibilities. Our minds are cluttered with decisions, appointments, tasks, projects, clients, and challenges from both our business and personal lives.

If you continue to clutter your mind, as small business owners often do, *overwhelm* sets in affecting the body with stress, anxiety, confusion, and most of all, lack of sleep.

At this point, small business owners go from clear AHA! moments to overwhelmed ARGH! moments.

Give me an amen if you have been there before.

I have experienced *overwhelm* in my business over the past 23 years. But nothing compares to the time in my business when I made a big shift in the services I offered.

During that transition, I became inundated with the amount of thoughts, ideas, research, contacts, communications, and advice I was gathering to start my new direction. All that information was stored on numerous legal note pads, sticky notes, printouts, email accounts, web browsers, computers, and mobile devices. My office was cluttered with piles upon piles of information. I couldn't see the top of my desk anymore.

My mind, too, was cluttered with trying to remember where I stored information, things I had to do, appointments to attend, and responsibilities to fulfill. It felt like there was no more room in my brain to think and there was no more room in my office to walk. How could anyone work like this?

Raise your hand if you have ever been down that path before! Frustrating, isn't it?

In no time, I began to lose focus and momentum, joy in work, and connection to my newfound purpose. Revenue was minimal. Productivity and growth slowed to a snail's pace. I was consumed by *overwhelm* in my business and personal life. Believe me, there were many sleepless nights.

Yep, I was stuck and going nowhere fast.

At that point, I knew I had two ways to address this issue. I could give up and just walk away (which I knew down deep wasn't an option for me), or I had to make some major changes to how I prepared, planned, organized, worked, and most of all, how I was thinking. I needed to take control of my business and regain the joyful experience of helping others with my services.

Being a problem solver by nature, I went on a quest to do just that.

TECHNOLOGY WITH PURPOSE

To support me through that process, I looked to technology for help. Not only was I looking for technology to help me manage and reorganize my work, I wanted it to help me be cognizant of my mind-game and spirit, and stay connected to my business purpose and life goals.

In order to meet my objectives, I experimented with a multitude of possible solutions and simplified down to three technologies—a digital calendar, digitally-assisted reminders, and an app called Evernote.

The digital calendar, which I had been using for years, now synced between all my devices, allowed me quick access to view, schedule, edit, and share appointments. It also allowed me to create event categories for each area of my life. I chose to create categories for Work, Personal, Family, and Balance. Each category has its own color. The first three categories you can figure out. The Balance category allowed me to reserve time for my personal well-being and growth.

Next, to unload my mind from trying to remember appointments, events, activities and family milestones, or when I had to perform a time or location-based task, I turned to digitally-assisted reminders. Digitally-assisted reminders are generated from apps installed on computer and mobile devices that notify you when an action needs to be taken.

Finally, one of the most important apps I discovered during the time of my business reorganization was Evernote. I credit most of my reorganization success to this app and it's still an integral part of my business and personal life.

If you're not familiar with Evernote, it is the Swiss-army knife of note-taking apps and often called the modern workspace or digital brain. I call it a productive thinking app because it helps me manage my thoughts, ideas, and work. Simply put, Evernote is the perfect place to gather, organize, store and search your important information. You can add anything you want to Evernote, from any of your devices, and be able to find it again in seconds from anywhere.

The best part about Evernote is it provides a workspace that allows you to work the way you think, create, remember, and process. Just what I needed!

HOW TO GO FROM OVERWHELM TO PRODUCTIVE FLOW - STRATEGIES AND TIPS

On the way to becoming productive, there were strategies and tips that helped me reduce *overwhelm* and increase productive flow. I continue to use these strategies to manage how I prepare, plan, work, and be mindful in my business and hope you find them helpful too!

The goal is to find at least one thing you can apply to help you be efficiently productive, reduce stress, be more mindful, and help you sleep better at night.

On my author page at the end of this chapter, you will find a link to a video where I show you firsthand how I utilize these strategies and the tools I use for my business and life. Come join me.

Preparing For A Productive Day

Have you ever thought about how you start your morning sets the tone for the entire day? The best way I learned how to prepare for a productive day is through a daily plan and consistent morning routine.

Review and Prepare

My productive day actually starts the night before. That's when I review and log what was completed that day so I can keep track of my progress. Then, I review my calendar to plan the next day. For me, starting the day without a plan is a guarantee for wasting time. Plus, a plan provides direction and avoids the continuous cycle of trying to figure out next steps, especially when there are interruptions.

Similarly, Joshua Zerkel, Director of Global Community and Training at Evernote, CPO®, shares "I prepare myself for a successful day the night before. I make sure everything I need for the day is packed and ready to go, and all I need to do is wake up and walk out the door" (Joshua Zerkel, personal communication, June 9, 2017).

Next, during review and prepare time, a list of tasks is created and time blocks are scheduled on the calendar. This helps me focus on the top five things needed to move a project(s) forward. If a task is time related, that task is scheduled on the calendar and an event alert is set as a reminder of the task.

Consistent Morning Routine

Each weekday morning I get up at 6am. The first thing I do is drink 2-3 glasses of water. Your brain tissue is 75% water. When you're not properly hydrated, your brain operates on less fuel, and you can experience fatigue. Next, I stretch to loosen my muscles, tendons, and joints (15-20 mins). Stretching is followed by deep breathing exercises to increase the supply of oxygen to my brain (10 mins). Combined with deep breathing exercises, I meditate to clear my mind and prepare it to focus. Lastly, I eat a healthy breakfast before heading to work.

I am not alone in having a consistent morning routine. In fact, many high achievers do. Matt Beall (CEO, Principal Broker, Owner Hawai'i Life Real Estate Brokers) shared with me he routinely begins his day with a meditation session, a one-hour light workout, and then either a jog on the beach, swimming, or surfing. Matt said, "I do all of that before I start my day, and I don't schedule any hard commitments before 10 a.m. or do anything else at the expense of my ritual" (Matt Beall, personal communication, June 6, 2017).

Daily Focus

During my Overwhelm period, I lost touch with my core authenticity, appreciation and joy for my business, people who were truly important to me, and my blessed life. Moving forward, I wanted a way to be mindful of those things on a daily basis.

Every morning, as part of my routine, I practice my "Daily Focus." The Daily Focus consists of giving daily gratitude statements, reading from a collection of my favorite inspirational quotes, reviewing my digital vision board, and checking my overall attitude before I begin work. The Daily Focus helps me stay grounded and be mindful of my business and life goals.

I use Evernote and its companion Web Clipper to collect, organize, and interact with my Daily Focus notes (files). In fact, I manage my entire morning process directly from Evernote.

Time-Action Management

The old cliché, *Take control of your schedule or someone or something else will,* is so true. I consider my calendar my most sacred tool because time is my most precious commodity. It's where I balance the time I spend on work, family, community, and me.

I love how Joshua Zerkel described the importance of his calendar - "My calendar is essential to my sanity. If it is not on my calendar, there is a slim chance it will get done" (Joshua Zerkel, personal communication, June 9, 2017).

One of the ways that most helps me work more efficiently is managing my actions differently. There are routine, but critical, actions I take each week to support my business and personal life. In order to make sure there is time for these actions, I reserve blocks of time on my calendar. Then each day, I review those blocked out times and schedule related actions. For example, every Monday I reserve time for marketing. It won't be until that day (or the night before) that I enter in a specific task—like *write blog article* or *post article to social media.* I call this *Daily Focused-Block Scheduling.* This method helps me make the most of my workday by assigning specific tasks to specific blocks of time on my calendar.

Anne Bachrach, The Accountability Coach™, is a big proponent of time blocking your entire day for best success, and recommends your highest payoff activities be blocked for first thing in the workday. "We all spend every second of our day the way we choose to spend it. You have to be very focused on what you're choosing to do if you're really serious about achieving your goals" (Anne Bachrach, personal communication, June 12, 2017).

50-10 Rule

Try using the 50-10 Rule (Burchard, Achievement Accelerator, 2016) if you feel like you're losing focus on work activities. On a daily basis, I schedule 50-minute chunks to work on the most critical tasks. I chose 50-minute blocks, because studies have shown that our peak focus span ranges from 45-50 minutes. During these blocks, NOTHING is allowed to happen except deep, distraction-free work. I turn on "Do Not Disturb" on my devices, and close email, text messaging, and social media apps. After 50 minutes, I get up from my work area and spend 10 minutes clearing my mind by taking a walk, stretching, or meditating. Rinse and repeat throughout the day!

Heather Mangold, Owner of Mangold Creative, takes this one step further. "If I have to be creative or think through a strategic plan or problem solve, it just won't happen in front of a screen. Instead, I'll sit on the floor of one of the collaborative areas in our office and map out my ideas on large sheets of paper" (Heather Mangold, personal communication, June 11, 2017).

Triggers

Consider using Triggers to help form good habits and establish routines. Triggers are preset statements or actions that aid us in reaching a goal. Michael Hyatt, Productivity Guru states, "Instead of relying on our decision making in the moment (when our willpower might be at its lowest), Activation Triggers lock in our decisions in advance" (michaelhyatt.com, 2017, How To Use Activation Triggers™ To Reach Your Goals This Year, para. 6).

Almost anything can be used as a trigger. I use the Reminder app, which is synced on all my devices, to display time-specific statements to trigger a response. For example, to check my attitude and energy level first thing in the morning, this message displays "How are you going to show up today?" I placed an anniversary watch from my wife on my desk to trigger inspiration for each day's work.

Reminders

Trying to remember every task and when to do it will definitely keep you up at night. Give your mind a break by using your calendar app, reminders app, Evernote, or any other app that will notify you when and/or where a task needs action. The advantage of using an app is that your reminders can be synced across all your devices, so the chance of seeing and/or hearing the notification is much greater.

Decluttering Your Mind with Brain Dumps

To declutter your mind, make it a practice to save thoughts, ideas, questions or anything else important to remember into a trusted source. I created a *Brain Dump* Notebook (folder) in Evernote to do exactly that, and my information is quickly accessible from any of my devices at any time or place. CEO Matt Beall shared, "Using a tool like Evernote just to articulate everything you need to be dealing with, without lifting a single finger on actually doing any work, will massively impact the feeling of *overwhelm*." (Matt Beall, personal communication, June 9, 2017).

Decluttering Your Physical and Digital Workspace

Clutter in your physical and digital work environment has a negative impact on the ability to think and work efficiently. After sifting out unwanted physical and digital information, I love using Evernote to capture, organize, and store all other information I want to remember. Paper-based documents, handwritten notes, business cards, sticky notes, and whiteboard notes can be scanned directly to Evernote with the camera on your mobile device or a physical scanner.

Web pages, email messages, photos, PDFs and any other digital documents can be saved to Evernote. I use Evernote to record anything audio I want to remember (i.e., client phone consultations). Evernote provides a system to keep my information organized, and its search feature allows me to retrieve needed information from any device or location. Essentially, I have all my information in one organized, accessible, and searchable workspace.

ACTION

Now it is your turn. What tweak could you make to minimize Overwhelm in your business and personal life? Start small, begin now, and enjoy the benefits of going from frustration, confusion, overload, resistance, uncertainty, and being stuck to simplicity, clarity, creativity, productivity, mindfulness, peace, growth, and a better night's sleep. Sweet dreams!

Why Small Business Owners Don't Sleep at Night
Glossary:

50-10 Rule: A method of working 50-minute distraction-free chunks of time to complete your most critical tasks followed by a 10-minute break to clear your mind.

Big Shift: A specific time in one's business or life when mindset, services, or responsibilities change based on personal, economical, geographical, technological, or new industry trends.

Brain Dumps: The complete transfer of thoughts, ideas, or knowledge about a particular subject from your brain to some other storage medium such as paper or a digital storage device (computer, smartphone, tablet, web-based storage service).

Daily Focused-Block Scheduling: A method to reserve blocks of time on your calendar to manage routine, but critical, actions taken each week to support your business and personal life.

Daily Plan: A written or typed plan, created on a daily basis, to help you organize your time better, prepare for specific actions or projects in advance, which will give a clearer mental picture about all the things needed to be done.

Daily Routine: Habitual personal-defined actions performed throughout each day to bring balance to your health, happiness, and productivity.

Digital Workspace: A virtual or electronic equivalent to the physical workplace.

Evernote: A digital workspace app used to create, gather, organize, store and search important information from any of your devices.

Evernote Web Clipper: An extension for your web browser that lets you capture and save directly to Evernote full-page articles, images, selected text, important emails, and any web page that inspires you.

Highest Payoff Activities: Activities, when completed, that make the most impact for moving forward on a project or goal.

Mind-Game: The thoughts, beliefs, and feelings you have that make up your reality and affects how you act.

Morning Routine: Personal-defined actions performed first-thing each morning to prepare you for a successful day.

Overwhelm: (noun) A modern term used by Small Business Owners (and general society) to describe the feeling of confusion and desperation experienced when their business/life seem to be spinning out of control.

Peak Focus Span: A specific amount of time that one can maintain the highest level of concentration on a particular subject or task.

Productive Flow: A state of ease and joy you experience when working and performing at the peak of your potential resulting in optimal output.

Productivity: The quality, state, or fact of being able to generate, create, enhance, or bring forth work output.

Time-Action Management: The act of taking control of your calendar by allocating the time it will take to complete specific task or action.

Triggers: Preset statements or actions that help form good habits and establish routines or aid you in reaching a goal.

Meet Brilliant Practicing Expert™ Dave Rebro:

Technology Therapist | Workflow Coach | Teacher | Integrator

His clients have dubbed him the "Technology Therapist." Dave Rebro's passion is to take a holistic approach to his clients' technology anxieties, frustrations, and overwhelm, and find solutions that best fit the way they think, learn, and work to help them reach their business and life goals. Dave's 25 plus years of technology knowledge and business workflow experience have contributed to his expertise simplifying technology and making it easier for people to understand and use. In that spirit, Dave is a teacher and coach at heart with a positive outlook on business, success, and life.

Although experienced in many technologies, Dave is an Apple Certified Support Professional/Integration and Certified Evernote Consultant.

DAVE'S SPECIAL INVITATION FOR YOU:

Learn firsthand how I utilize these strategies and tools for my business and life — come join me: www.Brilliant.DRCS-Solutions.com

DRCS Solutions

Business: DRCS Solutions

As a Technology Therapist, I help people believe in, trust, and build a productive relationship between their technology and their business and life goals. I take great pride and specialize in helping clients better leverage existing technologies, find new innovative solutions, relieve technology frustrations, build more confidence, improve daily workflow efficiency, work smarter, and make more money with the help of technology. Occasionally, I even talk clients down from the sometimes-scary technology ledge! I am an Apple Certified Support Professional and Evernote Certified Consultant with the emphasis on mobile technology solutions.

Website: http://www.drcs-solutions.com

Connect with Dave on these social accounts:

LinkedIn: https://www.linkedin.com/in/rebrod

Facebook: https://www.facebook.com/DRCSSolutions

Twitter: https://twitter.com/ipadexpertdave

YouTube: https://www.youtube.com/c/iPadExpertDave

iPad Tips and Tricks Newsletter: http://ipadexpertdave.com/

The Paperless Professional Newsletter: http://bit.ly/paperlessdave

Mobile App for *Brilliant Breakthroughs for the Small Business Owner* book series:
Find us on your App Store as: **BrilliantBizBook**

**Performance
Pillar 4**

PEACEFULNESS

Brilliant Breakthroughs for the Small Business Owner

Allow Me to Introduce Brilliant Practicing Expert™ Susan White by Maggie Mongan

Impeccability is the first word I associate with Susan White. I find this word accurately reflects Susan's approach to living and business. As a Licensed Clinical Social Worker, living and business are synonymous for her. I met Susan over 5 years ago and was astonished with her instantaneous capability to select words with precision. This precision is a reference to the laser-like accuracy of impact Susan has when she speaks.

We often hear, "words have power." The depth of this rings true when a master of conversation speaks. Susan's gift is deeply rooted in understanding people's beliefs and behaviors. Her conversations have literally saved lives.

When Susan speaks of how different aspects of our personalities impact our business's success or failure, she is spot on. With her impartial depth, Susan can peel back layers of illusions and falsehoods, which impede our success. Corporations engage with psychologists to support their leadership team's effectiveness. Susan serves Small Business Owners by helping them sort out their internal game, learn what is real and unreal, and create winning strategies and actions to generate favorable business results. Every Small Business Owner should have Susan on their team.

Hope: Out of the Shadows and Into the Light
by Susan White

Discouraged and broken, Steve stared at the stack of boxes sitting around him in disbelief. Cups n' Cakes had been the perfect bakery concept and he knew he was great at what he did. Years of praise confirmed it. People use to flock in for a cup of coffee and a sweet treat first thing each morning on their way to work. He knew his customer's names, personalized his service, and insisted his employees do the same. He was conscientious about costs, created a business plan, and experienced a positive cash flow soon after opening his doors. His vision of creating a small-town bakery had manifested into a successful venture.

Steve couldn't have been happier. Throughout the day, cookies, doughnuts, cakes, and pies would fly off the shelf creating next day demand for the same. That was then, and this is now – an empty store of neatly packed boxes. It all fell apart so quickly. Where did he go wrong? What could he have done differently?

Now, with all his hopes dashed – he reminisced. Disguising his shame with excuses, he waited for the movers to arrive. Today was the day the building needed to be empty, and that's how he now felt – empty and hopeless.

I'm fascinated with the abstract concept of hope, along with the role it plays in thoughts, feelings, and behavior – especially in business. This abstraction, when made concrete can make all the difference between success and failure to a small business owner. How does that happen? Scores of quotes, parables, and clichés can be found about hope, but what exactly is it? Don't we need hope in uncertain times and with uncertain circumstances, especially to handle our most challenging situations?

I find it impossible to explore the concept of hope without also addressing the shadow of hope. Defining and understanding the shadow, as well as how it may show up for each of us, is crucial to benefitting from hope. The ultimate objective is for hope to serve and provide us with a sense of meaningful support throughout life, as well as in business!

The shadow is a container within ourselves for all the thoughts, feelings, and qualities that we don't like, or want to hide, deny, or suppress. We fear and avoid being described as our shadow parts: loser, judgmental, lazy, stupid, selfish, or mean (just to name a few). We have learned these qualities are bad, negative, or wrong, and our energies go into suppressing, rather than embracing them.

As an example, we may hear ourselves say something like, "I'm not stupid". Although I must admit I have done stupid things. Haven't you? Stupid becomes an *aspect* of me. I begin to question, "How am I stupid," or "Is this thought or decision stupid?" The shadow can, and will, impact each aspect of who we are! It is our job to be fully conscious of how – and that can be a tall order!

The shadow is a trickster. When we deny shadow parts, we begin living in a fictional reality of who we are and how we show up in the world. Consequently, we believe if we control or manage everything, we'll be successful. It's denial of our shadow parts that stop us dead in our tracks and take us down a path of disappointment, or worse – financial disaster. This is what happened with Steve and his beloved Cups n' Cakes when another well-established full-service bakery relocated from a neighboring community to within a few blocks of his location.

The shadow of hope contributed to the destruction of Cups n' Cakes. Keeping in mind the concept of "shadow" represents qualities we don't like, or want to hide, deny, or suppress; reliance on hope limited Steve's leadership. He relied on hope in favor of reassessing his business and making much-needed changes to compete. He wasn't honest about the changing business culture, nor was he willing to adapt to new information. He "hoped" his bakery would "be fine." His fate was sealed.

On a much larger scale, we have seen this same thinking with big business. We've seen shadow beliefs demonstrated in the auto and building industries. This is most evident during times of recession, when big business must either radically adapt or risk bankruptcy. We've either directly or indirectly experienced shadow influences and consequences.

On a much larger scale, we've seen this same thinking with big business. We've seen shadow beliefs demonstrated in the auto and building industries during times of recession, when big business must either radically adapt or risk bankruptcy.

What allows shadow aspects to easily be identified within a small business is the frequency of decision-making demands – especially since they are made by one, or a couple of people. On the other hand, shadow aspects can easily be camouflaged within the corporate structure of policy and procedures since decision-making is typically reliant on expert consultants and a team approach. While a team approach creates checks and balances, a small business owner needs to be much more self-aware. After all, big business has the advantage of access to industrial psychology as an integral resource, whereas small business does not.

Being self-aware is not the same as being self-reliant. Decision-making in business is stressful, and personal leadership shrouded in shadow beliefs can negatively influence good decision making. Steve chose to see his business concerns as flaws, which in turn began to diminish his self-worth and self-value. He chose lies and fantasy in favor of truth. Initially, Cups & Cakes was a full-service bakery in a small town where the only competition was big box stores.

When Steve began, he was mindful about every move. Shortly afterward, he became complacent in his consistent growth and success. The shadows of success and competency that fueled his confidence to open his bakery in the first place, was now about to hurt him. He couldn't compete in the shadow of complacency. Without acknowledging his inner resources of brilliance, creativity, and vision, Steve was doomed.

All qualities have a shadow aspect: optimism, confidence, intellect, and perfectionism are just a few qualities that we may deem as desirable or positive. They too, have a shadow aspect. For example, a disowned part of confidence may show up as cockiness or arrogance when it becomes extreme. Initially, Steve relied on confidence and it served him as he charted new territory. Steve relied on marketing plans and met colleagues at Chamber of Commerce events, mixers, and business networking. His arrogance gave him the confidence to walk in the door when he didn't know a soul. In this case, "arrogance" fuels pride and becomes a valuable quality that is of service. Conversely, Steve's arrogance used him when he began to deny the threat of competition. He allowed his confidence to turn into cockiness and conceit.

Do you see how one isolated quality can either be valuable, or harmful, unless we are completely mindful and conscious of our shadow? As time went on, Steve's cockiness limited him in assessing the dangerous situation looming for his business. He was in denial.

As the tides of success began to turn, Steve refused to acknowledge his disowned fear and uncertainty about competition. He wouldn't ask for help, or admit he didn't know what to do. He wasn't willing to be vulnerable to new concepts. Sixteen months elapsed between the announcement of his competition's arrival, and their anticipated store opening. The shadows of complacency, comfort, denial, stupidity, and fear used him. Rather than acknowledging his shadow qualities, he chose to rely on past successes and arrogance – even in the face of evidence.

Embracing his shadows might have allowed Steve to rally. Rather, he succumbed to what he already knew. Author of the best-selling book, *Dark Side of the Light Chasers* (2000) and creator of *The Shadow Process*, the late Debbie Ford (2013) was often quoted to say, "Knowing is the Boobie Prize." What this means is, Steve knew how to begin his business, but not about reinventing his business, facing stiff competition, or using everything he learned since opening his doors. Instead, Steve did what he knew. The shadow vortex sucked him right into an empty room of boxes, which now contained all his hopes and dreams.

When we work with a qualified counselor or business coach to excavate our shadows, we can make the abstract concrete. We give ourselves the greatest gift of getting to know ourselves and how we function in a whole new way. Doing so creates a more in-depth understanding of our inner resources, which can help us handle our most difficult situations. Hope can, and sometimes must, shift and transform into an inner resource when we reinvent ourselves. Hope is evolutionary.

When we turn our backs on our shadow parts, we deny ourselves the possibility of turning dreams into reality. Instead we choose to wage an inner struggle which conflicts with what we claim to want for ourselves. If we live in the shadow of denial, refusing to acknowledge who we are and how we show up in life, we will keep attracting those very same qualities and experiences repeatedly. By simply becoming honest and taking action, we create new opportunities to know ourselves, and can have new experiences in our lives. As small business owners, we have a duty to do our own personal work in addition to honing our business skills.

To make peace with our shadow qualities, we must begin to accept them as part of ourselves. Acceptance is about feeling compassion, love, and appreciating all of who we are. We become whole.

One of my own shadows came to light while attending George Williams School of Social Work for my Master's Degree in Social Work. I was told by a Professor I would become a Hope Merchant. The notion triggered my insecurities instantly and I cringed at the thought. The notion of me being a Hope Merchant was daunting. I became angry and overwhelmed.

How was I supposed to create hope for others? Weren't they and their thoughts, feelings, and behaviors directly correlated to how much hope they did or didn't have? The denial of my own abilities, strengths, and gifts limited my notion of who I was. More significantly, this limited the possibility of who I might become! In academia, we have the luxury of inexperience. As a matter of fact, we are in that environment to address it! Through many years of both individual and financial investment in learning about myself, I have come to embrace the notion of Hope Merchant. I now see it as a powerful awareness and tool to support my work of serving others. You, too, can discover and learn to benefit from and use your shadows.

It takes courage to face our shadows, along with some good old-fashioned vulnerability. Hope isn't a substitute for hard work. It is not a strategy – especially a business strategy. According to Michael Lee, author of *Unusual Steps to Attract More Money into Your Life*, "The pleasure [success] you want to attain must be so gratifying – or the pain [failure] you want to avoid must be so agonizing – that you would put 100% of your focus and efforts to accomplish your financial goals" (https://www.stevenaitchison.co.uk/4-unusual-steps-attract-money-life/). Using hope requires we remove it from the shadows and trust our gut as we take actions. Hope is the fuel for perseverance in our lives. Aligned with vision, hope becomes a gravitational pull toward taking right action, not just a check mark on a to-do list.

Hope is the fuel we need to turn our dreams into reality. As small business owners, we deserve to do it justice by diving deeper and contemplate the polarities of fantasy and reality. When hope exists in the shadows, it can extinguish a dream in a flash because it limits or alters the truth. Then we begin living in a fantasy world rather than having a dream. We tell ourselves our perspective is the truth. When in reality it is nothing but a story – a lie we tell ourselves.

Maggie Mongan, Master Business Coach and Strategist, CEO and Founder of Brilliant Breakthroughs, Inc. defines hope as *possibility*. It is, especially when we use hope to open our eyes and our hearts to possibility. Opening ourselves to the unknown can be quite vulnerable and anxiety-provoking. We owe it to ourselves to also acknowledge the shadows of these qualities as well. To be human is to experience; to be an entrepreneur is to live the truth and act accordingly. That's one of the keys to making miracles happen. Sometimes not immediately, but miracles will eventually manifest.

It is clear the concept of hope is far more complex than previously imagined; yet, it isn't particularly complicated. Isn't hope a physiological need necessary to maintain a sense of stability in our society of anxiety? After all, sometimes hope is all a person has. Isn't hope also an essential component of life? When it isn't shadowed in an illusion of power and control, it is.

Using hope requires we take action, or rather active participation. When we hope for something and don't receive it, we mustn't simply look the other way and play victim. We owe it to ourselves to determine if we set ourselves up for failure by not utilizing all available resources.

Are you beginning to put together the pieces in which the shadow can wreak havoc on the most determined small business owner? As decision-makers in business, we must always be mindful of ways we either become victims or victors at our own hand.

Now that we've identified some shadow aspects of hope, how do we proceed with using it to create success in our small business, while simultaneously not allowing hope to use us in terms of denial, fear, fantasy, and blame?

Uncovering the shadow of hope means we are living with integrity. It reflects honesty and genuineness. We are no longer ashamed or embarrassed by who we are. Our self-worth soars and we become masters of our own destiny.

Becoming familiar with shadow parts isn't about perfection. It demonstrates integration of all qualities and becoming a whole human being. It's about removing some parts from the cesspool of judgment and labeling them as bad or wrong, along with coming to terms with all aspects of ourselves as having value.

The most remarkable thing occurs when we embrace our shadow qualities. Our self-esteem and self-worth isn't subject to the judgment of others. Personal transformation occurs as we learn how our perceived flaws can become our greatest assets. Using hope to support and guide us can create a shift in how we attend to ourselves, as well as our small business.

When hope materializes from the abstract to the concrete, it will lead and guide us in taking right action or creating new strategies as needed. In business, it may mean the difference between profitability or financial disaster. It is then, our dreams will endure as the foundation for growth, creativity, and evolution for our small businesses!

Hope: Out of the Shadows and Into the Light
Glossary:

Abstract Concept: A generic idea or understanding of something that is not concrete, and does not occupy space; a plan or original idea.

Acknowledge: Accept, admit, or recognize the existence or truth, importance or reality of a quality or circumstance.

Active Participation: An approach that enables individuals to be included in their care and have a greater say in how they live their life in ways which matter to them.

Business Plan: An outline or document explaining a business's future objectives and strategies.

Concept: Something conceived in the mind; an abstract or generic idea constructed from individual thought, perception, or experience.

Courage: The ability to do something that frightens an individual or strength in the face of pain or grief.

Denial: Failure to acknowledge an unacceptable truth or emotion or to admit it into consciousness, used as a defense mechanism; untrue.

Hope: A feeling of expectation and desire for a certain thing to happen; grounds for believing something may happen to help or save someone or something.

Intention: A process or manner to act in a certain way; a general desire or plan to accomplish something.

Integrity: The quality of being honest with oneself, as well as others, and having strong moral and ethical principles; sincerity, truthfulness, and trustworthiness.

Manifest: Display or show (a quality or feeling) by one's acts or appearance; demonstrate; be evidence of; prove.

Meet Brilliant Practicing Expert™ Susan White:

Licensed Clinical Social Worker | Integrative Life Coach

Susan White, MSW, LCSW and Integrative Life Coach, has worked in the Corporate World, Retail Management and Human Services. She's long been fascinated by personal transformation and human resilience – especially in the face of adversity. In 1993, she was told, "You've done well for someone with a substandard education." That back-handed compliment inspired her to pursue a BA from Judson College (1996) and MSW from Aurora University, George Williams School of Social Work (2001). Susan lives in her hometown of Antioch, IL with her husband and black lab, although she's lived in various locations throughout the Chicagoland area as well.

SUSAN'S SPECIAL INVITATION FOR YOU:

There's hope. Business Owners don't need to feel alone. Receive clarity today:
http://www.lifeskillsctr.com/

Lifeskills Center, Ltd.

Business: Lifeskills Center, Ltd.

After working at several non-profit agencies reliant on government funding, Susan White, MSW, LCSW, decided to create her own small business dedicated to helping people transform their lives. In January 2007, Susan founded, Lifeskills Center, Ltd in Antioch, IL. There, she helps adults face financial, relational or career concerns, mental health issues, divorce, death or any personal difficulties. Susan says, "We all face challenges we don't want to encounter, although viewing them as 'life experiences' often provides hidden opportunities to learn, grow and develop. That is the core of what Lifeskills Center and my work is all about."

Website: http://www.lifeskillsctr.com/

Connect with Susan on these social accounts:

Facebook: https://www.facebook.com/Lifeskills-Center-Ltd-331914257290/

Psychology Today:
https://therapists.psychologytoday.com/rms/prof_detail.php?profid=72780&p=1

Mobile App for *Brilliant Breakthroughs for the Small Business Owner* book series:
Find us on your App Store as: **BrilliantBizBook**

Brilliant Breakthroughs for the Small Business Owner

Allow Me to Introduce Brilliant Practicing Expert™
Lori Bonaparte by Maggie Mongan

If we were to jump into a time machine, chances are we'd find Lori Bonaparte doing exactly what she's doing today. Backward or forward in time, Lori's focus is steady. Maybe it's because she learned how to fly a plane from a WWII pilot.

Regardless of which timeline you want to focus on, Lori's genius helps you clear through your old beliefs that are holding you back. Through a unique process she's developed, she applies the best practices of neuro-linguistic programming (NLP) and Life Coaching techniques to help you gain clarity of what you truly want alive in your life. With Lori on your team, the two of you create a new path for you to actualize what you seek. Her approach is a well-balanced process of depth, simplicity, and safety for you to accept the *True You* that's been waiting to emerge.

I've witnessed Lori applying her expertise. I assure you she is nothing less than a Master Mind-Ninja. Swiftly she helps you get right to it. Lori supports you while you laugh and cry and then rejoices when you have your breakthrough. She also helps you create your new action plan to live into.

All Action, No Traction? Sometimes it's All in Your Head
by Lori Bonaparte

Congratulations! If you are a small business owner, you're part of the finest personal development program in the world. Like most, you may have unknowingly signed up for it. Yet, I assure you the program was inextricably present at the birth of your business, and most likely, even before then.

This highly customized personal development program holds both challenges and rewards. Both are necessary because it is through the challenges that the rewards come. The good news is there are plenty of challenges in business and this allows you many opportunities for rewards. Your customized personal development program holds particular challenges for you, within the four pillars of your business: PEACE, PEOPLE, PRODUCTIVITY, and PROFIT.

Your challenges within the area of PEACE will include elements of your past, present, and future.

Past: Do you experience familiar, negative emotions from your past that seem unrelated to what you are trying to accomplish? These seemingly minor emotions can become like a wedge between you and your reward.

Present: With all the hustle and bustle happening within a business day, are you able to remain present in the moment? Are you able to fully appreciate what is in front of you?

Future: Due to the nature of business, you will need to spend time considering the future of your business, both short-term and long-term. Does this bring excited anticipation or worry and anxiety?

Too many thoughts from the past or worries about the future can make being present in the moment extremely difficult. Yet, this is when the rewards are experienced best - in the present.

Your business will highlight relationships you have, or the lack thereof, with PEOPLE: customers, employees, vendors, partners, allies, competition, mentors, consultants, and coaches. Additionally, most small business owners find their business requires a fair amount of time and energy. You've probably noticed how relationships with your friends and family are affected by this.

You will have ample opportunities to consider how you present yourself to others and how you relate with them. There will also be plenty of opportunity to practice the handling of conflict, boundaries, and requests. Your business will consistently present you with situations to increase your awareness of the kind of leader you are, and the kind of leader you want to become.

A good leader is a master of productivity. Your way of thinking is unique to you and your level of PRODUCTIVITY has everything to do with how you think. Your uniquely designed, personal development plan will reveal how you internally access focus, clarity, self-discipline, motivation, and procrastination, which all directly impact your productivity.

PROFIT is usually a big reason for getting into business and is a necessity for staying in business. Your numbers will give you an external, unbiased, reality-based opinion of the past and current health of your business. Your ability to move through growth opportunities and challenges in the other areas will be directly reflected in your numbers.

This area is sure to present challenges with, and awareness of, your relationship with money. Since the money typically flows THROUGH your business and TO you, these challenges with money can show up in both your business life and your personal life.

This may be one of the biggest challenge areas for small business owners because it brings with it one of the greatest opportunities for reward; however, it's important to remember the reward extends beyond the money. According to well known, personal development coach and entrepreneur, Tony Robbins:

> In the end, money isn't what we're after. What we're after are the feelings, the emotions we think money can create: that feeling of empowerment, of freedom, of security, of helping those we love and those in need, of having a choice, and of feeling alive. (Robbins, 2014, p. 4)

Your business can be the platform to tap into those powerful feelings! You can leverage the personal development program already contained within your business to connect with your true self and lead a life of fulfillment.

When you are connected with your true self (the TRUE YOU inside) it becomes natural to utilize your gifts, talents, and strengths in pursuit of your intentional desired outcomes (or goals). In other words, you can use the best of yourself to go after what you want, and through the process, become a better version of YOU!

Intentionally pursuing desired outcomes through your business can be a source of financial livelihood and a form of self-expression. It can also evolve into a path to a fulfilling life (see Figure 5).

Figure 5.

True You in Action Discovery Path™

Source: Courtesy of True You in Action, LLC, True You Personal Foundation Program,
www.TrueYouInAction.com

The path to getting your TRUE YOU in Action starts with an initial Desired Outcome that you take Action on. If you don't take action on your Desired Outcomes, you will begin to feel Stuck.

As you attain Desired Outcomes and learn how to use your gifts, talents, and strengths to create the results you want, you will begin to feel Happy. If this is done well, you will experience Gratification. Conversely, if this is not done, you'll feel Dissatisfied.

As you intentionally create multiple Desired Outcomes, the momentum you gain will Empower you. Knowing you can create the results you want will add a sense of Freedom to your life. Conversely, if this is not done, you may feel Oppressed (as if life controls YOU, instead of the other way around).

When you reach a certain level of mastery in attaining your Desired Outcomes, a deep understanding of your unique and True Purpose will emerge. This leads to knowing you are living a Fulfilled life. Conversely, if this is not done, you could remain Unfulfilled.

Please note how gratification feels good in the short term and fulfillment is more long lasting. The father of personal coaching, Thomas Leonard offers a clear distinction: "Fulfillment vs. Gratification: To be fulfilled is to radiate your positive feeling consistently. To be gratified is to consume experiences, resources, or people. A fulfilling life sustains YOU; you don't have to manage IT" (Leonard, 1999, p. 124).

As a business owner, you are familiar with pursuing some of your desired outcomes; however, have you ever asked yourself, "What makes some of my desired outcomes seem unattainable or out of reach?" I've discovered there are three critical elements which are usually responsible for blocking intense traction toward any desired outcome you may have. They are: a lack of clarity, a disconnected WHY, and subconscious blocks.

A lack of clarity may occur when you haven't fully explored and clearly visualized your desired outcome. A great starting point is to visualize your desired outcome in positive terms. It's easy to think about all the things you DON'T want; however, your subconscious mind has a hard time processing negative input.

Your mind requires detailed, clear, and positive pictures of what it can help you create in the future. According to Richard Bandler, the co-creator of Neuro-Linguistic Programming, "When people create anything, they must create it first in their minds by imagining what it is going to look like" (Bandler, 2009, p. 8).

Another traction blocker is having a superficial or disconnected WHY. I'll admit, I did not fully appreciate the importance of this until I witnessed the power of a deep and strong WHY as I coached others. While the power of clarity is obvious from the beginning, the real power of a strong WHY reveals itself as you move toward your desired outcome.

It's important to understand how committed you are to attain your desired outcome and WHY you are committed to it. This is the root of your motivation. When the going gets tough, your WHY adds fuel to your motivation.

A strong WHY answers two questions: What is it going to do for you? What is it going to do for others? As you explore these questions on a deeper level, make sure MOST of your answers are in response to what it will do for YOU, instead of others. This will make it easier to tap into internal motivation later.

Here are some questions from Dave Buck, MCC, MBA, and CEO of Coachville Center for Coaching Mastery, to help you explore your WHY:

- What does winning look like for you?

- What would it mean for your life if you won on your own terms?

- If you did win, what would that mean to you personally?

- How would it impact the other areas of your life?

- What is the real opportunity for you here?

- Why do you want to do this?

- How will achieving your desired outcome create a life of self-expression and purpose?

- How will it change lives for the better?

- How will it change the world? (Buck, 2014, pp. 34 - 36)

The last critical element which may be responsible for your lack of traction is subconscious blocks. Your subconscious is extremely powerful because it's involved in everything you do! It also operates outside of your awareness. Dr. Matthew James of *The Empowerment Partnership* shares some news about brain use:

> Do you remember growing up and hearing that we use only 5-7% of our brain? Researchers are revising that belief. Now they say that we use ALL of our brain but we only use 5-7% consciously. It's not that we haven't tapped into the 95% - we have. We're just not conscious of it (James, 2012, p. 61).

If we only use approximately 5% of the brain consciously, wouldn't it be good to know what the other 95% of our brain does? Richard Bandler explains it like this: "Your conscious is the part of your mind that analyzes, criticizes, and thinks logically all day long. Your unconscious is where all your memories are stored and where your wisdom, creativity, and problem-solving capabilities reside" (Bandler, 2008, p. 3).

How is this relevant to your business? One of your subconscious mind's jobs is to protect you. It comes up with brilliant operating instructions to do just that. However, there could be effective operating instructions that it created when you were a young child which have turned into subconscious blocks, hindering your traction today.

Let me give you an example. Let's say when Mike was seven years old, his parents decided to throw a business party at home. Mike really enjoyed it. As more adults came, he started telling them the best jokes a seven-year-old could concoct. At some point, his parents told him, "Be quiet. Stop talking. These people aren't interested in what you have to say. They didn't come here to listen to you." He felt ashamed that he disappointed his parents. His subconscious mind leapt into action with operating instructions to protect him, "If I'm quiet, I won't have to feel ashamed. People aren't interested in what I have to say anyway."

Fast forward to adulthood, Mike is a successful business owner who wants to take his business to the next level. He's an outgoing guy who enjoys talking to people. He knows a part of what he needs to do to reach his desired outcome is to give presentations to groups of people. Yet, any time an opportunity comes up to give a presentation, he gets a *gut feeling* that it's best to avoid that situation. Those operating instructions he created as a seven-year-old have now become a subconscious block holding him back from the desired outcome he currently has for his business.

Your subconscious mind has remarkable functions that directly impact your business. For example:

- It maintains instincts and generates habits.

- It sometimes represses memories with unresolved negative emotions in order to protect you.

- Later, it presents repressed memories for resolution (as seen in Mike's situation).

- It stores and organizes your memories, and is also the domain of emotions (Advanced Neuro Dynamics, Inc., 2016, p. 18).

One of the most profound things I've discovered about the subconscious is that under the guidance of a skilled practitioner, your subconscious mind has the capacity to release a subconscious block very quickly, even within the course of a single conversation!

If you've read this far, I'm certain you are a committed business owner. You have willingly accepted the daily challenges, which present themselves as part of the personal development path, that you must travel to get to the rewards within your business. It's important to remember that although these challenges seem as if they're within the environment – most of the time they are not. In reality, a vast majority of the time, they are contained within your mind.

If you would like to further leverage your business to get your TRUE YOU in action, a good place to start is with the action steps below. You may have unknowingly signed up for the finest personal development program in the world; yet, once you're proficient at creating your desired outcomes, you won't want it any other way.

YOUR ACTION STEPS

1. Decide on a current desired outcome that you'd like to attain.

2. Define your desired outcome with clarity. Continue this process until you have a visual image of it and then write it down in detail.

3. Write your answers to the above questions regarding the creation of a deep and strong WHY.

4. Increase your awareness of any subconscious blocks you may have. You can do this by thinking about the actions needed to attain your desired outcome. Notice if you feel any internal resistance when you think about doing them. It is normal to feel some apprehension when you're stepping into new and unknown territory; however, if you notice a feeling of dread, you may have discovered a subconscious block.

5. Take at least one small action, TODAY. This tells your mind, "It's time to start!"

All Action, No Traction? Sometimes it's All in Your Head
Glossary:

Clarity: A detailed and clear definition regarding a desired outcome.

Desired Outcome: What you specifically want to do, be, or have. A goal.

Relationship with Money: The way in which you are connected with money, as influenced by your thoughts, emotions, behaviors, beliefs, and attitude about it.

Subconscious Blocks: Thoughts, emotions, and behaviors which are incongruent with a desired outcome (usually outside of your awareness).

WHY: A specific and clearly defined understanding of what attaining your desired outcome will do for you.

Meet Brilliant Practicing Expert™ Lori Bonaparte:

Personal Development Coach | NLP Practitioner | Serial Entrepreneur

Lori Bonaparte is a Personal Development Coach (certified with the International Coach Federation), NLP Practitioner, and Serial Entrepreneur. She is on a personal mission to help others get to the heart of their TRUE YOU within, and learn the skills needed to practice living a life that is intentionally created.

She believes that each and every one of us was created with a purpose and a personal mission. By utilizing our unique gifts, talents, and strengths to attain our desired outcomes in life, we become more connected with our purpose and feel more fully alive.

LORI'S SPECIAL INVITATION FOR YOU:

Download the video training "7 Steps to Get Your TRUE YOU in Action" at http://www.TrueYouInAction.com

TRUE YOU IN ACTION

Business: True You in Action, LLC

True You in Action is committed to inspiring you to connect with your true self, get your TRUE YOU in action, and live the life you love. This is done by clarifying your desired outcomes in life, and then helping you to utilize your unique gifts, talents, and strengths in pursuit of them.

At True You in Action, the combination of Positive Psychology, Provocative Coaching, and Neuro-Linguistic Programming are weaved together and delivered via interactive videos, workshops and coaching to help you learn the skills needed to practice living a life that you intentionally created.

Website: http://www.TrueYouInAction.com

Connect with Lori on these social accounts:

Twitter: https://twitter.com/loribonaparte

Facebook: https://www.facebook.com/trueyouinaction

Mobile App for *Brilliant Breakthroughs for the Small Business Owner* book series:
Find us on your App Store as: **BrilliantBizBook**

Brilliant Breakthroughs for the Small Business Owner

CONCLUSION

By now I'm sure you noticed our team of Brilliant Practicing Experts™ is overflowing with best practices and unconventional approaches to help you succeed in 21st century small business success.

We hope you have built out a plan (strategy) to take actions from whichever chapters will best serve you now. Each quarter come back and find some more techniques to improve your business's performance.

REMEMBER: This book isn't a *read it and place it on the shelf* book! Just as Jeff Koser, CEO and founder of Selling to Zebras, stated "Mark this book with a highlighter and refer back to it for a year – when the next version comes out!"

This book is dedicated to you. It is designed to make your job easier. The only thing I'd like to add is how to make this book work for you:

- Apply the strategies and techniques discussed here.

- Accept each authors' invitations on their Author Page.

- Engage with the authors via their social media accounts.

- Download our Free Mobile App: **BrilliantBizBook**   Why? Each author will have extra and ongoing support there for you.

- Go to amazon.com and let us know what you found useful and then let us know what you'd like to learn in our next book (2018).

Also, some of you have already asked, "What's in store for next year?" and "Who will the new round of Brilliant Practicing Experts™ be?"

"Guess you'll just have to wait and see" is the answer. Maggie Mongan, Your Anthology Leader, masterfully works to make sure there is no overlap of expertise and each of The 4 Performance Pillars for Small Business Success™ are well represented.

START HERE: Follow the above checklist and begin shining brightly!

Brilliant Breakthroughs for the Small Business Owner

AUTHORS' COLLECTIVE BIBLIOGRAPHY

4 Unusual Steps to Attract More Money Into Your Life - Retrieved August 30, 2017, from https://stevenaitchison.co.uk/4-unusual-steps-attract-money-life/

Abraham, M. (2015). *The entrepreneur's solution: the modern millionaire's path to more profit, fans & freedom.* New York: Morgan James Publishing.

Albert Einstein Quotes. (n.d.). Retrieved July 27, 2017, from http://www.brainyquote.com/quotes/authors/a/albert_einstein.html

Bandler, R. (2009). *Get the life you want.* Deerfield Beach, FL: Health Communications, Inc..

Buck, D. (2014). *Play-Two-Win Method* [Coach Training Materials from Coachville - Center for Coaching Mastery].

Chang, Amber (2017, June 8). Personal Communication [Telephone interview].

Chaplain, Teubel, Lisa (2017, August 7). Personal Communication [Telephone interview].

David Kocol, LLC, Kocol, D. (2017, June13). Personal Communication [Telephone interview].

Dixon, M., & Adamson, B. (n.d.). *The challenger sale.* New York, Portfolio Penguin.

Evernote Corporation, Joshua Zerkel (2017, June 09). Personal Communication [Telephone interview].

FocalPoint Business Coaching of Wisconsin, Weseman, Jason (2017, June 22). Personal Communication [Telephone interview].

Gary Vay-Ner-Chuk (@garyvee) · Instagram photos and videos. (2017, July 7). Retrieved July 7, 2017, from https://www.instagram.com/garyvee/?hl=en

Hawai'i Life Real Estate Brokers, Matt Beall (2017, June 07). Personal Communication [Telephone interview].

I Have a Dream, Martin Luther King Jr. : Dr. Martin Luther King Jr.: Free Download & Streaming. (n.d.). Retrieved July 27, 2017, from https://archive.org/details/MLKDream

James, M. B. (2012). *Find your purpose: master your path.* Kailua-Kona, HI: Advanced Neuro Dynamics, Inc.

James, M. B. (2016, September). *The Integrative NLP Practitioner Training Manual* [NLP Practitioner Training Material through The Empowerment Partnership]. Kailua-Kona, HI: Advanced Neuro Dynamics, Inc.

Kim, W. C., & Mauborgne, R. (2016). *Blue ocean strategy: how to create uncontested market space and make the competition irrelevant.* Boston, Massachusetts: Harvard Bus Review Press.

Konrath, J. (2006). *Selling To Big Companies.* S.I.: Kaplan Publishing.

Koser, J (2017, July 18). Personal Communication [Telephone interview].

Koser, J., & Koser, C. (2009). *Selling to zebras: how to close 90% of the business you pursue, faster, more easily, and more profitably.* Austin, TX: Greenleaf Book Group Press.

Laurinavicius, T. (2017, May 09). The importance of photography in personal branding. Retrieved August 19, 2017, from https://thenextweb.com/creativity/2017/04/09/personal-brand-deserves-high-quality-photography/#.tnw_38wrXyfg

Lechter, S. L., & Reid, G. S. (2012). *Three feet from gold: turn your obstacles into opportunities.* New York: Sterling.

Leonard, T. J. (1999). *The portable coach: 28 sure-fire strategies for business and personal success.* London: Simon & Schuster.

Mangold Creative, Heather Mangold (2017, June 11). Personal Communication [Email interview].

Michael Hyatt & Company, LLC, M. H. (2017, January 11). How To Use Activation Triggers™ To Reach Your Goals This Year. Retrieved June 05, 2017, from https://michaelhyatt.com/activation-triggers.html.

Mongan, M. (2017, February 2). Simplify Small Business Success Program. Retrieved May 22, 20017, from https://academy.brilliantbreakthroughs.com/

Mongan, Maggie (2017, April 30). Personal Communication [Telephone interview].

P. (2014, May 14). [STUDY] Different photos of the same person leave wildly different first impressions. Retrieved August 19, 2017, from https://blog.photofeeler.com/same-face/

Proctor, B., & Gallagher, S. (2016). *The art of living.* New York City: Tarcher.

Ray, James Arthur (2017, July 21). Personal Communication [Telephone interview].

Robbins, A. (2016). *Money, master the game: 7 simple steps to financial freedom.* London: Simon & Schuster.

Santino, George A. (2017, July 7). Personal Communication [Telephone interview].

Sinek, S. (2009). *Start with why: how great leaders inspire everyone to take action.* London: Portfolio/Penguin.

The Accountability Coach™, Anne Bachrach (2017, June 12). Personal Communication [Telephone interview].

The Burchard Group, Brendon Burchard (n.d.). The Achievement Accelerator. Retrieved January 15, 2016, from http://brendon.mykajabi.com/products/the-achievement-accelerator.

Vengreso, Gerbyshak, Phil (2017, July 5). Personal Communication [Telephone interview].

Wargo, E. (2006, July). How Many Seconds to a First Impression? Retrieved August 19, 2017, from https://www.psychologicalscience.org/observer/how-many-seconds-to-a-first-impression